IMPOSSIBLE DECISIONS

Doreen Padfield is an experienced counsellor and social worker who has spent some years teaching disabled children and then working in a children's hospital. She oversees the spiritual development of students of counselling at St John's College, Nottingham, and is a freelance counsellor. Married with four grown-up children, she lives in Essex. Her daughter, Deborah Padfield, is the Editor of *The Friend*, the Quaker journal, having previously worked as a freelance writer and for the Methodist Division of Social Responsibility.

Impossible Decisions

MAKING DECISIONS
WHEN NO WAY
SEEMS RIGHT

Doreen Padfield

With Deborah Padfield

First published 1993
Triangle
SPCK
Holy Trinity Church
Marylebone Road
London NW1 4DU

British Library Cataloguing in Publication Data
A catalogue record for this book is available from the British
Library.
ISBN 0–281–04679–4

Typeset by Inforum, Rowlands Castle, Hants
Printed and bound in Great Britain by
BPCC Paperbacks Ltd
Member of BPCC Ltd

To Tina and Karen
with love and grateful thanks
for all they have taught us

Contents

Acknowledgements

We would like to thank all the people who have made this book possible, especially Tina and her family.

Grateful thanks also to Richard and to Jenny Pardoe for their unfailing support.

The quotation of T.S. Eliot on page 40 is from **Burnt Norton** *from* **Collected Poems** 1909–1962 *(1963)*, used by permission of the publishers, Faber and Faber Ltd.

1 | *What is the problem?*

Have you ever been in the situation where whichever decision you take, whatever you do, it is wrong? Not just a mistake – but wrong; against all your instincts, so that part of you is howling, 'No, no – I can't do that!' The situation where, twist and turn how you will, there is no alternative to doing something which horrifies you?

It is not a good place to be, that place of impossible decision. I have been there myself. I have talked and worked with many people who have been there far more agonisingly than I. This book is written out of that experience. It is written in the hope that it may be helpful to others who are facing impossible decisions, or who are trying to support others in that same desperate, lonely place of confusion.

What was it that set this book in motion? It was my contact with Tina, Joe and little Jamie, and through reading the diary which, at my suggestion, Tina wrote as she faced and went through the process of aborting her longed-for baby son. When Tina gave me this diary to read I found it an incredibly moving testimony to the courage and honesty with which she had faced her terrible dilemma. With Tina's agreement I showed it to my daughter. She too found its honesty, and the issues which it raised, both moving and challenging.

We started thinking about the stages through which Tina had passed on her journey of decision; about the difficulties of each stage, and about the things which had enabled her to take her decision and to survive it as a whole, unembittered, loving person. I started thinking about the other people I have known in the course of my work, who in very different circumstances had similarly faced the impossible. Deborah, who like me is a Quaker, has like me talked with many people in many different situations, and as she is a writer, she started writing. We have worked together on this book. The professional experience is mine; the act of writing is hers. It has been a process of prayerful thinking which we have undertaken together. At times the process has been complicated – as at the point where she writes of my experience of parenting her, an anorexic teenager. But the partnership has added to the richness of the experience.

So: what is the background which I bring to this book? I have come to it by a twisting path – more by chance than design. Like many women, I spent most of my young womanhood as a wife and mother. Once my four children were all at school – the youngest, Deborah, still at the local primary – I wanted to return to work. I found myself teaching physically disabled children almost by accident, the Barnardo's home being in our home village. The children were a lively bunch who found much delight in the ordinariness of our cookery lessons and a wicked joy in pastry fights in the corridor. I was not overwhelmingly popular with the head teacher.

Those children needed a sense of home; they needed love. I found my contact with them very rewarding. It made me realise more clearly where I needed to go. A very close friend encouraged me; I went to Middlesex Polytechnic and did a degree in social sciences together with the certificate of qualification in social work. It was hard, returning to academic work, but I loved it. When I graduated, I became a psychiatric social worker. It was enormously fulfilling work. I was so privileged to work amongst those families, talking to those people about their lives, their memories, their hopes and fears.

After several years, I moved to a children's hospital. Here, my clients were even more varied – socially and racially. I found myself working a good deal with the nursing staff who had to handle such incredibly traumatic cases yet who had to retain their buoyancy in order to give the kind of care which was needed. There were people of very varied faiths and people of none. But we worked together and in difficult times many of us found a strong unifying bond. Perhaps I should call it a common sense of dependency. And we learned to laugh together, even in impossible situations. It was not heartlessness. It was a simple need to break the tension, to let the awfulness go for a while. We needed to see the comedy which so often bubbles just under the surface of tragedy; to acknowledge and take joy in the good things, small and great, which can so easily pass unnoticed when we are tired and stressed.

Was my religious faith important to my work? It was not a question which I asked myself most of the time. Certainly it was not a subject much discussed amongst the staff. Sometimes I wondered why on earth I was doing this work – so tiring, so endless, so pointless in our inability to 'solve' people's problems. But I knew that it had not been a choice. This kind of work had chosen me.

Not that I was particularly 'good' at it. Much of the time I felt devastatingly inadequate. I was more than capable of putting my foot in it, of being extraordinarily slow to see the implications of what someone was telling me or mindbogglingly tactless in what I said. But, warts and all, I had to be there. And I think it was similar for others of the staff, certainly for some of the cleaning staff; badly paid and physically tired as they were, they would often perform those extra little acts of kindness, of generosity, for either staff or patients which mean so much.

And prayer? I am not good at formal prayer. I lost, a long time ago, the ability to speak to God as I had been brought up to do in childhood. But, oh, yes – plenty of prayer, heartfelt prayer, in the sense of that wordless reaching out for help; the sense of being held, all of us being held, in strong arms. I would remember the story of the man who went to give an important lecture. On the way, he lost his notes. 'When I left home,' he told the packed auditorium, 'only God and I knew what I was going to say. Now only God knows.' I know the feeling.

It does not matter at what stage in my work I met Tina and her family. The section which follows now is the diary which she wrote, before and after her abortion: her impossible decision. The rest of the book is not the story of Tina, Joe and little Jamie. It is the story of the process through which Tina passed; the process through which so many others I have known have passed, together with their friends and families. The process of deciding between two impossible actions and of learning to accept forgiveness for what they had to do.

2 | *Tina's Diary*

Tina was in her late 20s when she became pregnant for the fourth time. She and her husband Joe already had three daughters, Samantha, Corinna and Jade. Corinna had cystic fibrosis.

Tests showed that the baby was a boy and that he, too, would almost certainly develop cystic fibrosis. As Tina wrestled, agonised, over whether or not to have the pregnancy terminated I suggested that she might keep a diary, to write out her thoughts and feelings, her anger and grief, her guilt and longing. She did so.

Much later, Tina asked me to read what she had written. I was so moved by it that I suggested that others facing similarly devastating decisions or seeking to help their friends through such dilemmas might be helped by reading it.

For the sake of privacy, all names have been changed. Tina herself chose the pseudonyms given to herself and her family.

Tuesday January 17th 1989 (9 weeks 2 days)

First visit to the local hospital at 9.30am. Had a scan. I saw its little head and arms and feet, it was the best feeling I had ever had. (Susan came with me, were there till 2.30).

Thursday January 19th 1989 (9 weeks 4 days)

Second visit to local hospital, saw Mrs Groves (doctor). Had first examination, everything went alright. (Susan came with me. 9.30-1.30pm).

Friday January 20th 1989 (9 weeks 5 days)

Today Joe took me to the specialist
hospital (9.00am), where we met Jane
Tennant, who took blood from Joe, Corinna
and myself, so they could do the test to see
if my baby had cystic fibrosis; they also
needed part of the placenta, so they made an
appointment for another city hospital.

*Thursday January 26th 1989 (10 weeks 4
days)*

Today Joe took me to the city hospital for
test (10.10am). I had a scan, then they put
a tube inside me and sucked some of the
placenta out. I had to rest for a week, or I
could lose my baby (it was not a very nice
test to have done). Was there about two-
and-a-half hours. Deanna had Jade for me
then I went home to bed. I had to wait two
weeks for test results.

*Saturday January 28th 1989 (10 weeks 6
days)*

Deanna came round and told me the phone was
not working, so she took me back to her
house because I had been getting pains in my
stomach.

*Thursday February 2nd 1989 (11 weeks 4
days)*

Joe took me to the local hospital
(10.10am). Was told to take one more week's
rest.

Thursday February 9th 1989 (12 weeks 4 days)

Went to local hospital 10.45am. Results still not in.

Friday February 10th 1989 (12 weeks 5 days)

Got a phone call from Jane Tennant. The blood tests were taking longer because my blood was not right, so they had to X-ray my blood. The results should be in on Monday.

Monday February 13th 1989 (13 weeks 1 day)

It was 10.30am. The phone rang and it was Jane Tennant. She told me that the tests were 96% that the baby had c.f. I asked her if she knew what my baby was, she said it was a boy.

Tuesday February 14th 1989 (13 weeks 2 days)

Dr Edwards came round at one o'clock. She told me all the trouble that could happen to my little boy. Then she said I should really decide what to do this week because time was going on, and the longer I leave it the harder it will be.

Wednesday February 15th 1989 (13 weeks 3 days)

Doreen Padfield (the health visitor) phoned and was very helpful. She said whatever I decide to do, I will be doing the best for my son and the girls and of course my husband. She also said I would be feeling damned if I didn't have him and damned if I did. They were the truest words I have heard in a long time.

Thursday February 16th 1989 (13 weeks 4 days)

Got up and dressed and me and Joe took the kids to school. Then I left them there and went to see Dr Edwards and told her to go ahead with the arrangements. She phoned me back later that morning telling me I had to go to the local hospital on Monday 20th February 1989 at 8.30am, Ward T6, and that I would be there overnight (come home Tuesday 21st).

Monday February 20th 1989 (14 weeks 1 day)

I never got much sleep last night thinking, am I really doing the right thing for my baby and my family? I feel so much love for my unborn child, so much guilt inside for what I am about to do, will I ever be able to live with myself after all this, and I still don't know what to do for the best. I think to myself,

1) What type of life would my son have?
2) Would he have bad chest problems?
3) Bad bowel problems?
4) Would he be in hospital most of his life?
5) Would he thank me for bringing him into this world?
6) Would I see him in so much pain and regret bringing him into my world?
7) Could I stand back and see him wanting to run and play, and maybe he could not do it?
8) How would he feel, and me, when I tell him he could never be a natural father?

9) How do I tell him that c.f. children
   live day to day, not knowing how much
   time they have on this earth?
10) And the BIG question is, do I LOVE HIM SO
   MUCH that I would give him up?

Before I can go into hospital, I have to
know all the answers to my questions. YES, I
DON'T WANT MY SON (JAMIE) TO LIVE LIKE THIS,
I DON'T WANT HIM TO SUFFER. I LOVE HIM SO
VERY MUCH, IT HURTS SO MUCH TO GIVE HIM UP.

I don't think he would thank me if I
brought him into a world of fizzy and tablets
and hospitals. And how would he feel if he
found out that I had the choice to keep him?

I will never know what Jamie would have
been like, but I will never stop loving him,
or wondering if I was right or wrong. I will
always remember the day he was taken from me
(Monday February 20th 1989) and the day my
son would have been in my arms (Sunday
August 20th 1989) for me to love and to have
shared that love with his dad and his three
sisters.

He will always be in my thoughts and in my
heart. Because if things had been
different, life would be one great big ball
of happiness for all the family.

I feel empty inside and a pain that no-one
can ever feel, and a very big need to love
and hold my son in my arms and tell him I
love him very much. I just wish things could
have been different.

Monday February 20th 1989
Joe woke me up at 7.30am. The sun was
shining by 8.05am and I remember thinking,

why doesn't it rain, because that is how I felt, sad, unsure, and not knowing what is going to happen to me. We arrived at the hospital at 8.25am. We went in a lift to Ward T6, where they asked us to wait. At 9.00am they took me to a room number 8 (16b), where a lady doctor asked me questions:

1)   My name
2)   How many children I had
3)   How many had c.f.
4)   What was their age and sex
5)   Any illness in the family
6)   And would I sign the consent form

Then she told me to put on a white gown. She took my blood pressure and listened to my chest. Then another doctor took me to a treatment room, where they put a jelly type capsule inside me. This hurt and I was told this was to make the womb soft. Then I was taken back to my room, where Joe was waiting for me. We never said much but I wanted him to take me home. But he told me we were doing the right thing.

At 10.45am a nurse came in and put a paper cap on my head then a porter came in and put me on a trolley. I looked at Joe and cried, I knew now that Jamie was going and never coming back. I told Jamie I loved him all the time while I was crying. They put me in a lift to the 8th floor, where I had to stay in a hall till the next lady was out of the theatre. I was so scared, just lying there helpless thinking, I want my baby, I love him, don't hurt him. Please don't let

anyone hurt him. A black nurse came over to
me and said, 'Stop that crying, you made
your decision, that's why you're here.' And
I told her I loved my baby I don't want him
to go. I had no real chance to keep him, he
has c.f. After that she was quite nice to
me.

Then they put me in a room, put some pads
on my chest and gave me an anaesthetic. I
remember saying, 'Don't hurt my boy please,
don't let them do any test on him. Just let
him be. Tell him I love him please.' Then I
was out.

12.00pm. I remember coming round and
seeing a drip in my hand, seeing a clock.
Crying out, 'I love my baby.' Then I said to
a nurse, 'This drip is hurting me, take it
away.' She said, 'I can't do that', so I
said, 'I'll do it, then,' and she turned and
said, 'You do that, Mrs Williams, and you
will bleed to death, so it is up to you.'
After that I remember crying for my lost
child and going back to sleep. I was woken
up again to be told I was going back to my
room. The time now was 1.00pm. When I got
there I was told Joe had gone home. I just
cried myself back to sleep. I was woken
every fifteen to twenty minutes because they
had to check how much blood I was losing. I
was losing quite a lot, so the drip had to go
quicker, I had two bags of fluid to help stop
the bleeding. By this time the pain in my
stomach was pretty bad, they gave me a
needle in the backside.

At 4.00pm Joe came up, he never said much
but he looked at me for a while then looked
out the window, he would not talk to me,

just kept saying, 'What do you want me to say?'. He left at 7.45pm. I cried myself to sleep, but nurses kept waking me up. I had pains all night. But all I could think about was my baby and how much I have lost.

And no matter how much time goes by I will never know if I did what was best for my baby that I never kissed or held or showed him how much he was loved.

I just hope he will know I loved him from the amount of time I lay on my bed talking to him and telling him just how much he meant to me.

Jamie I love you so much.

Tuesday February 21st 1989

My drip has been taken away and I am allowed to get up and have breakfast. Feeling empty inside, crying inside I went to the breakfast room and had a drink where ladies were so mean about people who had terminations that I went back to my room and cried again. When I pulled myself together I had a shower and got dressed, feeling dizzy and very uncomfortable. I sat in the TV area, waiting for Lyn Jones to take me home, got home about 10.45am. Susan came down and sat with me. When Joe came home from work he took me down to my mother's, where I am staying for the rest of the week.

Tuesday to Friday 21st to 24th February 1989

This week I have tried to put on a brave face, but the pain in my stomach hurts quite a bit. When I go to bed I can't sleep, I just seem to lie there crying, telling Jamie that I do

love him, asking God to look after him. I
don't want to upset Mum and Dad but I just
can't seem to sleep at all. I just feel like
crying all the time. When Joe comes down I
don't cry, I just sit there trying to stop
the tears from coming down my face, it's
hard, because everything on TV seems to be
about babies, and mostly boy babies. When I
see them I just want to cry and wish my baby
was still inside me. If I had three wishes I
think I would ask that my three girls would
stay healthy and well, that me and Joe stay
happy in love and together, and that I had my
baby Jamie in my arms on 20/8/89.

I'm going home tomorrow. I hope I can go on
without upsetting anyone. I seem to feel I
want to be on my own and just cry or think
about life. I don't want to see anyone, I
don't really want to speak to anyone. I know
I have to be strong for my little girls, but
it doesn't seem to matter during the day,
it's just night time, I can't sleep because
of all the guilt, and a feeling of
emptiness. I don't know how I will be going
to school seeing people pregnant and small
babies everywhere. I just hope I can cope
with all I will go through.

I love Joe very much and hope we may have
another child, but I have a very strange
feeling that it will never happen. And the
trouble with this is, I am never going to be
happy until I have a baby in my arms.

My nightmare

I lie awake not making a sound, tears are
running down my face, right or wrong the
pictures keep going through my mind of what

I did to my unborn child. I close my eyes that's when it starts. I am lying in a hospital bed waiting to be taken upstairs to the 8th floor. Joe is standing by the window. When a nurse and a black porter come into the room, they put me on to a bed trolley. Tears are flowing down my face, I'm thinking, God help me through this, please look after my baby. The lift doors open, now we are going up, 7th floor then 8th floor, the lift rings and they wheel me out. I lie there in the hallway for maybe ten to fifteen minutes not knowing what is going to happen to me, then they push me into a little room and tell me everything is going to be alright. They give me something to sleep. I ask them, 'Don't hurt him will you, tell him I love him very much.'

Within an hour I'm awake but I see lots of shelves full of bottles, big bottles with little things in them. I look closer and I see they are all tiny little babies with names and dates on them, I go along the shelves and then I see it: baby Williams, male fetus with c.f., 14 plus weeks old. I scream but no-one hears me, no-one hears my screams of pain to see my baby Jamie on that shelf. Then the dream gets worse, I am at home now looking after my three girls and tuck them into bed, kissing them twice each, the second kiss I give them is for Jamie the baby I wanted so very much. I go downstairs and close the door, and I see a big blue and silver pram in my living room. The pram seems to be moving, but tears run down my face, and I go and sit down, watching this pram moving slowly. I get up

and go to the pram and pull the covers back,
I scream but again no-one hears me. Inside
my pram is Jamie in a bottle looking at me
and crying. Will this nightmare ever stop?

I loved my baby more than anyone will
know. I did what I did for him.

But I miss that feeling of life which made
my baby and me happy. Now all I feel is
emptiness, cold and deprived of the one
great thing in life, a baby kicking inside
of me. No future children could ever take my
unborn baby son, Jamie, away from me.

I just hope as time goes by it will be more
easy to live with. I'll never know if what I
did was right, I can just hope it was.

God, I am so down, and putting a happy face
on when I can for my kids and husband and
friends and family. When inside I am
falling apart and thinking, can I really go
on like this?

Sunday March 19th 1989

Dear Diary, I would have been 18 weeks
pregnant today. It seems to me that Sundays
aren't very good days because it makes me
think how far gone I would have been. The
night time comes so quickly and I am still
having my nightmares. I lie in bed with Joe
beside me; he's fast asleep and I'm lying
there next to him in tears, I get up, make
myself a drink and walk the floors. Then when
I feel my eyes won't stay open I go to bed
again.

Monday March 20th 1989

Got up today, took the children to school,
met Pat and walked home together. She asked

me round for tea. When we got there she was looking after a little baby boy of 5 months called Thomas, and while I was there she kept giving this baby to me. Tears were fighting to come down my face, but I would not let them, all I kept thinking was, I'll never hold Jamie in my arms, rocking him to sleep.

I started to wish this baby was mine, but he is nothing like my baby would have been. My baby would have been blond, with big brown eyes and the best looking baby around.

When Thomas went to sleep I put him down in his pram and made an excuse to leave, as I walked home the tears flooded down my face, I felt guilt, hate, love and injustice of what I had done to my own baby. I felt gutted/dead but when I see my girls I think, well maybe one day Samantha/Corinna/Jade will have their little baby brother or sister.

And I might get over this tragedy.

Saturday March 25th 1989

Today has not been so bad, the children are keeping me busy and I am trying to catch up with the housework. It's now 12.20am, I'm awake, my eyes are sore, and I think I have just got my period - the first one since D-Day. The pains I am having remind me of the day I had my termination. I feel like crying, but tonight I'm not going to cry. I have my little ornament beside me, who I now class as Jamie the little boy I never got to hold or kiss. I talk to him morning and night, and any time no-one is there. I tell him how much I love and care about him, and I hope that there is life after death and that God is looking after him, because I believe that when you die, you meet up with all the family and loved ones who are now not with us.

Please keep my Baby safe up ther
I love him so much ♡

Sunday March 26th 1989

Today I would have been 19 weeks, I would have been feeling my baby's first movements, its first real sign to the world that he was here. Funny that I come on when my baby would have been moving about inside of me.

Life has a funny way of showing how much different things mean to different people, like, I'm thinking what my body would have been like and felt like, my husband has been behaving like it never happened and just can't wait to have normal sex again. I think to myself, wouldn't it be nice if he just once said, how he misses not having his son, it should be something we share together.

What if time doesn't heal the pain? What if what I thought was right was really wrong. Do I say, well we all make mistakes, or am I really a killer like I feel?

The day comes
The day goes
The sun shines
The rain falls.
Happy days
Sad and empty nights
Come and go
Life goes on.
For some
Life ends
For others -
Babies born
Babies grow
Some you see
Some you don't.
Are you right
Or are you wrong,
Who's to say,
Today you're happy
Tonight you're sad.
Your mind
You don't understand.
You need
You want
But don't always get.
Life is strange,
But is life fair
Who am I
I don't know
I feel empty
Unhappy
Unloved

They say time
Is a great healer
But I don't know
For sure
I'm alive on the outside
But feel dead on the inside!

Sunday April 2nd 1989

20 weeks, I would have been half way through
the pregnancy and I would be feeling my
baby's kicks inside of me. (Funny, Deanna
is going to have her baby very soon now. I
can't seem to be happy for her.)
   Went to the park with Joe and the girls.
Saw Deanna there with Sally and Michael. I
watched Michael and was sad that I will
never see Jamie running in the park or
hugging me like Michael did Deanna. I had to
fight to keep the tears inside. I wish I
could share my feelings with Joe, not that I
blame him for any of this but because I
think it would bring us together. It's now
April 2nd and I am still having my dreams/
nightmares about my termination. I hope one
day they will go away.

My poem

Our precious bundle
Wrapped in blue
Will always mean the
World to us.
His Daddy's pride
His Mother's joy
His Sisters' love
Will always shine through.

We never got to meet our son,
Just a picture on a scan.
But we will picture him
In our minds.
Wrapped in blue
Full of life.

I never held my baby boy
But I did cradle him in my womb.
No-one could see him
But he was there
My little bundle,
Just lying there inside of me.

We hope his life goes on in the next world,
That God will look after him, for us,
Till the time comes when we shall meet
again.
I believe in life after death
So one day our family
Will be all together
A bigger family
Than I have now.

For who knows
What life has for me
And my children
And their children
And their children
But I know we will all be together
One day.

3 | Caught in a trap

'She said that I would be feeling damned if I didn't have him and damned if I did. They were the truest words I have heard in a long time.'

Not all of us meet, in our own or friends' lives, dilemmas as terrible as the one expressed above – 'damned if I do and damned if I don't'. But all the same, most of us know that awful feeling of 'heads you win, tails I lose'; whatever I do will be the wrong thing. The smallest problems can become major bugbears which haunt us in the middle of the night and pounce on us unexpectedly in the middle of the day. With which in-laws should we spend the first Christmas of our marriage? Now my daughter is sixteen, should I try to insist I know where she is going, or will that make things even worse?

Some lucky people can take the line that once they have decided what to do, they will just relax and live with their decision. Others of us worry at the problem, while it gets bigger and bigger and more and more insoluble in our minds. The smallest difficulty can grow until it dominates our lives; and it is rarely much help if our friends just tell us not to be so silly, to stop worrying. It is much more helpful if they can, somehow, help us to sort out the aspects of the problem which are important, the advantages and disadvantages of each solution, the possible compromises. Nearly all of us know, in one form or another, the desperate feeling of fighting a problem which has grown too big for us to handle, and which has no 'right' answer. It is this kind of dilemma which Tina, and many others I have met, were facing.

I had first met Tina and Joe six years before. Their middle daughter Corinna had cystic fibrosis. This meant twice-daily physiotherapy to release the mucus which formed on her chest, allowing her to cough it up. The disease affects children in different ways, but it tends to mean that their carers must exercise extreme care to ensure that they do not catch the chest infections which, ultimately, kill many of them. A severely affected baby can spend most of its first year or eighteen months in hospital – which, of course, means that the parents, and particularly the mother, need to spend an immense amount of time there also. No-one knew what Corinna's life expectancy was. Some have lived into adulthood, and even, very occasionally, have had children. Many die either in childhood or in adolescence, but their life expectancy is improving enormously, as the result of new research and painstaking treatment by the medical teams.

At five years old, Corinna was beginning to play her mother up, refusing to take any notice of her. She was an intelligent and attractive child, as most c.f. children seem for some reason to be. Tina, not surprisingly, was finding it hard to be firm enough with Corinna – a problem which Joe could see quite clearly. Inevitably, Corinna's behaviour was affecting her two sisters, Samantha and Jade. Samantha was then seven, a lovable and rather serious girl, aware of her responsibilities towards her two younger sisters. Jade was three, much more demanding than Samantha, and inclined to be rather jealous of the attention necessarily lavished on Corinna. When we met on one occasion, Tina told me about the situation, and together we managed to think out a more manageable way of life.

A little later, Joe and Tina came again. Tina was pregnant. It was a shock. Where would another child fit into their small two-bedroom house? Joe was working as a skilled mechanic, but there was no chance at the time of moving to a bigger house. On the whole, though, they were very happy about the baby – but for the fear that this child also would have cystic fibrosis. Tests were done. There was a 96% chance that the baby, a boy, would have c.f.

Tina was utterly shattered. Though he showed it far less,

so was Joe. They had so wanted a son. Nevertheless, Joe was sure that they should have an abortion: that to have another c.f. child would have devastating effects on their own relationship and on the three girls. It was already hard enough for the family, coping both with Corinna's c.f. and with its long-term prognosis.

Tina was far more confused. She needed desperately to talk through the decision, and we spent some time doing so. I encouraged her to write out her thoughts and feelings. It was the uncertainty which was so difficult: if the baby were severely ill, then Tina would be torn in two, between the hospital and the rest of the family. And what kind of a long-term prognosis could there be for the child? What kind of a life would he have? But perhaps he would not be so severely affected . . .

I cannot remember saying the phrase which Tina wrote in her diary. But I do remember the long conversation we had when she was making up her mind to have the abortion. To have the son she longed for – and maybe to see him grow up a prisoner of endless hospitals and physiotherapy, at who knows what cost to her husband and daughters? To kill the child, who was so much a person to her already? Whichever way Tina turned, the horror and the guilt were unbearable. She wanted to cry out, 'Somebody help me!' 'Somebody take this decision away from me!' – but nobody could. She was caught in a trap, and she could not get out.

It is hard to watch someone suffer in this way. So many of us have been in a position like that of Tina and Joe, or of the friends and family who surround them. The marriage break-up, where one or both partners are agonising over whether it is better for their children to grow up with two unhappy and quarrelling parents, or to see their father or mother move out. The dreadful decision as to whether to have a seriously handicapped baby adopted: what is best for it and for the older children? The operation which will keep a family member alive, but as a cabbage, unable to recognise or respond to people. The unbelievable nightmare when one family member is accused of sexual abuse: how can one sort out what to believe, and what will be the action least damaging both for children and adults?

Those entangled in these kinds of problems find it hard to hang on to any certainties about the 'right answer'. There is never any way of knowing what will happen, or what might have happened. And there is no way that a watching friend can take the awfulness away – that very helplessness is, indeed, a dreadful burden for that friend. But there are ways of at least lessening the loneliness of this kind of hell.

Issues like divorce, abortion and perhaps above all suicide, can challenge us on several levels at the same time. We often think we know how we stand, morally and religiously, on major dilemmas like these – until we are actually faced with them, either directly or in the person of a close friend or family member. It can be a terrible shock to discover that what we thought we believed, clearly and firmly, can be shaken to the foundations by the test of experience. More than a shock; it can be devastating, tearing us apart with confusion and guilt. It is then that we discover that we are two beings: a religious and moral person, with strong and sincere beliefs; and an ordinary human being, with capacities for love and grief, for hatred, anger and despair, for whirlwinds of conflicting emotions and thoughts, which we had never suspected.

This discovery is not fatal to the journey of faith; indeed, it is part of it. It crops up in major religious writing down the centuries, St Paul's amongst them. And it points us to the need for prayer, in which we learn to merge our humanity and our faith in one coherent whole. After being confronted with doubt and confusion, our faith is not the same. It has been given a chance to grow, to be informed by compassion and humility. We learn that the doubt, the confusion and the passionate question 'Why?' are necessary parts of faith. They are born out of the struggle for love and justice which is the action of God in us.

This is my experience. For others it does not work that way. Many who have suffered this kind of hideous dilemma find that it destroys their faith, or confirms them in their unbelief. The idea of a loving, almighty God seems so far from their experience that they reject it, often never to return to religious faith. They are unable, in their bitter hurt, to let that faith grow and change; to come to a different understanding of God and God's relationship with us. If this happens to one of your friends, or to yourself, how do you respond? It is very tempting to try to put up the protective shields, to wall out the problem by saying, 'Well, abortion is wrong', or 'Suicide is wrong', so all this grief or terror or loneliness or despair must also be wrong, not to be given way to. But that is a bit like putting up an umbrella when you are already soaked through. Saying, 'I'm not wet' will not make me any drier. These emotions are part of our human make-up; they are behind the protective shield – under the umbrella – already. Somehow our faith has to take account of that. And so does our response to our own and our friends' agonies. Just how to respond is something we never fully know; we just have to carry on learning by experience – sometimes bitter, sometimes unexpectedly joyful. After all, learning about human beings is a lifetime's task!

Someone faced with this kind of agonising, insoluble problem, needs a friend who will recognise the reality of the pain and the desperate responsibility. Most of us tend to shy away from those in real pain, afraid, partly, of saying the wrong thing. We avoid talking about it, or we say in effect, 'There, there, it's not so bad really . . . Worse things happen at sea.' Indeed, I find myself wanting to say that kind of thing out of self-protection. When a situation is so unbearably painful, I *want* to minimise it. For my own sake, I want to tell myself and the other person that it will all turn out all right.

But that is dreadful for the sufferer. To belittle the decision in that kind of way makes the sense of being trapped, the loneliness and the fear far worse. Tina needed to know that I recognised just how impossible her decision was: that whatever she did, she would 'be' guilty. But she also needed to know that in spite of that fearful guilt, she would not be outcast, she would still be human, she would still be loved and loveworthy. And, knowing her guilt, struggling with it, she would also be innocent. That is the central paradox of being human in a world full of conflicting, irreconcileable demands. 'Forgive us our trespasses, as we forgive those who trespass against us . . .'. Sometimes I think this is the prayer most central to a Christian belief. It recognises that as we are humans living so close to one another, we will constantly be hurting each other. It accepts that fact, yet it accepts also that we often do not want, or mean, to do such damage. It is the prayer for those who recognise the way they affect others, yet who still love life.

When I first met and really recognised the kind of dilemma faced by Tina, I realised that I had to take the implications of my friend's impossible decision seriously; I had to help her think the issues through as they affected the other people concerned. This kind of thinking is desperately difficult and painful, but it is also important if your friend is ever to emerge from the maze of confusion, guilt and anger. It was because Tina was so clearly and courageously aware of what it meant either to kill Jamie or not to kill him that, over time, she was able to accept her own responsibility for the decision and, slowly, to let go of the endless, irrational guilt. She could accept that in that impossible situation she had taken the best decision available to her at the time. She had done her best.

At the same time your friend, running round in the endless circle of horror, may sometimes need to be reassured that there will be a future, that this decision is not going to destroy either herself or those she loves, that their strength to survive, and love, and laugh, is stronger than she, in her confusion and desperation, can believe. It is a fine line, this, to let your friend know that you recognise and respect the true awfulness of the situation; yet also to add a tang of reality when it is needed, preventing her from imagining herself to be the 'Beast of the Apocalypse', destroying the world by the 'unforgiveable sin'. This is something which I have realised from my own personal reactions to grief: that however genuine and overwhelming the pain, we are still capable of over-dramatising ourselves and our situations. Partly this is because we cannot bear to feel the full force of the pain, but it is remarkable how powerful our human sense of self-importance is.

The grace of laughter is a real gift of healing. So often in my experience, laughter can spring out of nowhere in the most agonising situation – and it can be a real lifesaver. It was Karen, above all others, who taught me that. I first met her when I was a student social worker in East London. She was then twenty-four years old, and twenty-four stone in weight. She worked, in her own erratic way, as a prostitute.

Karen's life was a continual saga of unforeseen disasters and complications – it was one long insoluble problem. She had been thrown out by her parents as a child, and had grown up in Local Authority care. At sixteen, she had to leave her children's home, with nowhere to go, and she turned to the only profession for which she was qualified. No-one was inclined to believe Karen when she said how little she ate – until she was taken into hospital. She then had to undergo a hideous series of operations to help with her steadily growing weight problem. At one stage, most of her intestines were removed to try to prevent her absorption of water. It did not work.

On many occasions, when the situation was so bad that my mind could no longer cope with the complications, I caught Karen's eye and both of us would start laughing helplessly. There really was not anything else to do. But, of course, this was only possible because she knew that I knew just how desperate her situation was; just how real the pain which she suffered. She knew how much I respected the battle which she was continually fighting. I have shared the same release of laughter with other people since – but always on the same basis of a mutual respect and recognition.

Karen was a trier. However impossible her current problem, she would have a bash at it. But it was a little difficult to see how she was to tackle the repainting of her living room, when it finally became too dilapidated even for her. Karen had no money for paint or workmen. Her partner was never likely to get round to starting the job. Karen was far too fat to bend over, even to tie her shoelaces. Reaching up or standing on a chair were both too dangerous. But she could manage painting between thigh and eye levels . . .

Karen's partner brought home, from various sources, assorted pots of paint. Avoiding the furniture as best she could, Karen emblazoned the walls with a bold central stripe of canary yellow. Confronted with this when he came home, her partner finished the job: warm orange above, and sky blue below. It may not have been the ideal answer, but it was the best Karen could do. Her indomitable courage and resourcefulness in bad times taught me a lot, and I have found those qualities in others again and again since. One of the great bonuses of my work as a social worker has been the amazing assortment of people for whom I have developed, and felt returned, a very deep affection and respect. I have gained so much from these encounters.

4 ║ Knowing the facts

'Dr Edwards . . . told me all the trouble that could happen to my little boy.'

Tina was lucky in one respect: she knew very well what cystic fibrosis was like. The doctors were careful to tell her the likely odds of Jamie being a healthy child. She had seen other cystic fibrosis children, and knew the long hours of physiotherapy, the difficult diet, the pain and the uncertain life expectancy. The doctors could not tell her how seriously he might be affected.

Even so, it was hard for Tina to apply the known facts to her own situation. There are the endless hopes. Perhaps we will be in the lucky four per cent, and he will not have it. Perhaps it will not be too severe, he will not have to spend too long in hospital, his life expectancy will be good. Then there is the longing for the facts to bend a little. Perhaps, somehow, we will be able to cope. Maybe, somehow, it will become easier, not harder. We are all well acquainted with this kind of dreaming, half-persuading ourselves into a belief which we know, really, is fantasy. It weaves into our thoughts over the most everyday of subjects: if I look again in my handbag, that urgent letter will be there – I just did not see it; maybe I did misread that telephone bill. Sometimes, with big shocks, we need this kind of fantasy. It can cushion the blow, give us time to gather our resources before tackling the reality.

Because, beneath the momentary fantasy, there are those heavy drumbeats of reality, reminding us that this is pure wishful thinking. They reminded Tina of her own responsibility towards her daughters and her own health and strength in the future. What would be the impact on the other three of another handicapped child, diluting her attention even more? Tina would go round and round, sometimes fighting the facts, sometimes struggling to acknowledge them. All I could do was to listen, sometimes reflecting back to her what she was saying so that she could hear herself more clearly; and to give her the affection and respect which she needed.

Anna, whom I had met a little earlier, was less lucky when she in turn faced an impossible decision. She did not have Tina's agonised but clear awareness of the surrounding facts. Anna was diabetic, and blind. She and her husband had tried again and again to have a child, and Anna had had a series of miscarriages. Finally, in her mid-thirties, she conceived again, and went through the first few months without problems.

The doctors did tests, and warned Anna and Mike that the child would be handicapped. But Anna could not bear the thought of abortion. They had so longed for that child; they had been taunted with hope by former pregnancies, only to be desolated by yet another miscarriage. Deciding actively to end a pregnancy – to kill the child – just was not a possibility for them. They decided to go ahead with the pregnancy.

From the hips up the baby, a boy, was perfect. His pelvis and legs were undeveloped. They were like a tiny doll's, and would always remain dwarfed; no one knew how much they would grow. Anna and Mike came to the agonising conclusion that, given Anna's blindness, they would have to give the baby up for adoption. I was called in at this point, as the couple struggled to live with the pain of parting with their child, after so long a wait for him. I have seldom met such a long-drawn-out anguish of bewildered grief.

For Anna, the cry was, 'Why didn't they tell me?' If she had known just what this handicap might be, if she had had the real implications spelt out to her, then she might have made a different decision about the abortion. At least one would have known the odds, and would not have headed so unknowingly down this no-through-road. I don't know whether the doctors really did fail to spell out their findings to Anna and Mike. It may well be that the couple did not really understand, or take in, what they were being told. We have all had the experience, in times of stress, of listening to someone and realising too late that we have not heard a word they have been saying. It is precisely when I personally most need to listen that I am liable to wander agitatedly off into all kinds of minor side-turnings. I have needed a friend with me sometimes, to listen soberly to what I was being told, who is then able to fill me in on the gaps when, bewildered, I emerge from the lawyer's office or doctor's surgery. It reminds me of that awful moment when you're just starting the driving test and the examiner says, 'Turn right', and you can't think which is left and which is right – the mind just goes blank! Anna and Mike needed to talk over their dilemma with someone, chewing over what the facts would mean to *them*, in their situation. At the time they had to make a decision, they had no such friend.

Maybe the doctors were not specific enough, did not paint the picture clearly enough. Doctors are very familiar with the illnesses which they see constantly; they know the whole picture. It is sometimes easy for them to forget how strange and alien this world of sickness is to other people. They do not always realise how carefully, how clearly and how repetitively they need to paint a picture of the facts and their implications for the patients and their families. This is not a criticism of doctors. It is the same for many professionals: they can find it hard to describe effectively what to them is so clear. Indeed, it is the same for all of us. It is hard to believe that the other person does not know or understand what to us is so blindingly obvious.

Of course, there is also the ostrich syndrome. Faced with unbearable, or even uncomfortable, situations, most of us have the impulse to bury our heads in the sand. This decision is too bad, it is impossible, let me hide and it will go away. Maybe Anna and Mike were, to some extent, being ostriches. Contemplating the very possibility of deciding to have that baby aborted was unbearable. Only, of course, the implications did not go away.

Glenda's mother and father, whom I met when Glenda was about six months old, were prime examples of advanced ostrich syndrome. Glenda had developed a monstrous growth on the side of her neck. Not only was it hideously unsightly, it was also beginning to grow inwards, preventing her from swallowing. There was an operation, and the growth was removed.

But it came back. Glenda's father neither loved nor disliked her. She was a girl, and he was indifferent to her. He was equally indifferent to his wife, who acted literally as unpaid servant to himself, his son and his brother, and to his mother, the real head of the household. With such an active policy of repression by her husband and family, Glenda's mother felt unable to take action. They ignored the growth, until when a social worker called she found the eighteen-month-old Glenda thin and frail, simply starving to death. The second operation was also successful, but it was a close-run thing. In delaying action, Glenda's mother was only doing what many of us find ourselves doing. We try to hide, and avoid an active decision, allowing the decision passively to take itself. Most of us do so under far less pressure than had built up on this woman.

There are real dangers in this, even if the outcome is not so drastic as in Glenda's case. Such a 'letting happen' can remain with us like an alien force, a 'fate' which at that crucial moment dominated our lives. This sense of not having been in control, or of failing to take control, can become a source of bitterness, colouring and distorting the rest of life. To some extent, I think Mike and the blind and diabetic Anna genuinely had not taken in what they were being told about the degree of handicap to expect. But to some extent they simply could not cope with hearing – did not want to know. 'Can't' and 'won't', in this kind of situation, are closely linked. There is no point in saying, 'Of course you can.' We learn to recognise those who, in real crisis, have reached the limits of their strength. I think that Mike and Anna had reached their limits. But it meant that they carried with them the terrible bitterness of the, 'Why didn't someone tell me?' Their decision had been taken in the dark.

With Corinna already in the family, suffering from cystic fibrosis, Tina and Joe had no comparable protection of ignorance in taking their decision. But it was a bit easier for them, afterwards, to accept their own responsibility for that decision. They had looked at the situation and at its implications, and in the light of those had taken as clear a decision as they could.

What can a friend do at this time? It is so tempting for anyone close to those facing this kind of dilemma to try to protect them, colluding in the ostrich syndrome. That can be most true of family members. It is hard to see one's partner suffer; parents long to shield their children. 'Of course you have no option, of course you can't cope with having the child' – or, 'with having an abortion,' they say. And sometimes that is a sound instinct, the instinct which knows when a pain is too hard, and that the sufferer just needs to hide in the dark and not face the fact that this is a real choice. For Mike and Anna, abortion never presented itself as a genuine option. Therefore, they did not seriously think through what the implications would be if the child was seriously handicapped. But even when, as for Anna, one of the options is too terrible to be contemplated, in factual terms it remains a real choice. Afterwards, when guilt or regret start biting, it is something of a lifebelt to be able to recall that there was some rational element in this decision. It was not 'only' the gut response of an anguished heart, but also made sense in the cold light of day, given the circumstances as they then appeared.

In some circumstances, thinking through the available facts just is not a practical possibility. I think, actually, that that was the case with Anna and Mike. So deep was their distress that they literally could not think about the possibilities. But that is not always true: quite often, people are far stronger than they think they are, or even want to be. When faced with discomfort or pain, most of us are capable, consciously or unconsciously, of doing a bit of manipulation. At one end of the scale is that appalling headache when there is going to be a really tough day at work. It may be an entirely genuine headache . . . but it is remarkable how conveniently it can be timed. Or there is that unthinking remark to Mum when she rings, about how difficult it is going to be managing with the children tomorrow. We quite sincerely do not mean to drop hints, but unconsciously, that is what we do. It can be quite entertaining to spot when we are going in for a bit of manipulation, and it is certainly no bad thing to recognise that this is something we all do. It might help us to be a bit less rude about other people when we spot them doing it!

At the extreme, there is the suicide threat. 'If he leaves me, I'll kill myself.' 'If I had my child fostered, I'd die.' These are not likely to be just wild and whirling words, meaning nothing. They reveal genuine desperation. But while recognising this, we need also to recognise the unconscious exaggeration which is quite probably also going on. That is not easy to do. And being with someone in that kind of anguish, recognising the depth of the agony without being swept up into it, is not easy either. It is at this kind of time that I need to remember, silently, that both I and my client are in the hand of the Spirit – strong, understanding, and endlessly compassionate – a source of strength always available to us.

In this kind of crisis situation I have found by hard experience that if I mentally refer to the textbooks and use a technique I have learned to help me reach out to the other person, it does not always work. That kind of mental alertness, the impulse to treat the situation as a pattern which my cleverness can resolve, gets in the way of real attentiveness. The 'I' gets in the way. If I can listen silently and receptively, I find that when the moment comes I can sometimes say things I did not know. We look at each other in surprise, and with some emotion. Saying that thing, whatever it is, can be an immense release for the other person; and, indeed, for me too.

There are also times when there is nothing left to say. We sit together for a little time, I do not know how long. A powerful, indefinable bond joins us together in that stillness. In the silence, something very healing can happen.

This kind of attentive listening has a firm place amongst the reconciliation skills used to bring together two opponents in a dispute. Much in formal or informal counselling is indeed very like reconciliation work. A tough personal problem will generally involve a collection of people, each of whom sees the situation in a different way, with different priorities. There is your friend, tied up in knots with tension and ready to react with anger or grief at practically any suggestion. Then there are, maybe, the doctors, lawyers, social workers, minister; the children, partner, parents; each of them with their own picture of what is happening and what any decision would entail. To speak to a desperate father, trying to paint for him a picture which he can understand of what these other parties are saying . . . it is a delicate, sensitive job. And then again to speak to them, if that is appropriate, trying to portray for them just what their words mean within the hell in which the father is imprisoned. And to judge when, how far, at any moment, the father is capable of being challenged. People are incredibly fragile, and one has to recognise the limits of strength. But, paradoxically, they are also incredibly tough.

I have realised again and again that there are no 'simple facts' in these situations. What is 'true' depends on who you are, what your expectations, fears, longings and hurts are. The 'facts' are only a part of the story – quite a small part. It is what those facts *mean* to people which is really significant. For Tina, the abortion meant the killing of a child she already knew as a person; her husband Joe knew no such person, and the implications of the decision were therefore very different – though I learned not to underestimate his pain. But as Tina wrote, 'Life has a funny way of showing how much different things mean to different people . . .'. Tina, gradually, realised what was going on, but the kind of non-communication they initially experienced in their pain can split marriages wide open. Joe, though silent and un-comprehending, was eventually able to accept the depth of Tina's distress. Over time, they were each able to see, to some extent at least, the other's understanding of the experience through which they had passed. That is a process which has been continuing since the last entry in Tina's diary.

A magistrate trying to decide whether or not a child should be taken into Local Authority care has to take into account these differing pictures of the 'facts', as portrayed by different parties in the dispute. She or he has to look at the outward evidence of the parents' situation and treat-ment of it. What may to the parents seem the greatest poss-ible care, may to the magistrates appear totally inadequate. Which is the 'right' assessment? Sometimes magistrates will have to take a decision which the parents cannot under-stand as being just or fair; the perceptions are too different. If any of your friends or family are in this kind of situation, then you will have to judge your response carefully, re-sponding to them afresh each time you see them. Some-times they will just need to explode with their anger, their frustration, their incomprehension and their desperation. They will need you simply to hear and accept that medley of emotions. At other times, they will be able to hear, maybe little by little, your understanding of the magistrates' pic-ture of the situation; the viewpoint which made them de-cide the way they did.

Both personal experience and cultural background colour our standards of judgement. I have sometimes found myself in the situation of trying to interpret to parents just how the situation appears to the authorities; or to the authorities just how this family operates. My contact with twenty-four stone Karen led to the first of many encounters with authority. A prostitute with no stable partner, a highly uncertain income and a major and handicapping health problem needed to work hard to explain her adequacy as a mother to Social Services and thence to the magistrates. I had to paint for them a picture of a very 'different', but genuinely loving and strong family. All credit to the magistrates that they accepted that picture.

Not only, though, is there conflict between the views of the different parties struggling to understand the 'facts'. There is also conflict within those parties. We can be divided against ourselves. Both Tina and Anna, with her blindness and tragically handicapped baby, were torn in two by the two sides of their dilemma: now listening to the voice of abortion, and convinced by the necessity for it; now listening to the voice of the child, and unable to contemplate parting with it. There is something in it of the nightmare quality of having two people passionately, angrily, emphatically shouting their two radically different convictions at you at the same time. You just want to put your hands over your ears and hide. You certainly can not disentangle what is important to each, or weigh them against each other. Having heard one, you then need quietly to hear the other, so the two can be looked at side by side.

The job of the friend might be to help do this. It works differently for different people. Sometimes I have simply talked with them, trying with them to disentangle the different strands of thought; to work out what they are really saying, what their real priorities and major concerns are; to follow through some of the implications of what they are saying, and their impact on the future, on the family, on themselves. Sometimes, as with Tina, I have encouraged people to write down their thoughts. It is amazing how putting them on paper can help to clarify them. Seeing them coldly in black and white sometimes has the effect of shock treatment. 'Of course I don't mean that', or, 'can't do that.' Writing a web chart can be good, in which there are arrows connecting actions and their effects, interlinking them all. Or putting down a list of 'What is really important', and adding to it, underlining or bracketing items through the day or the week, according to the priorities that emerge.

Sometimes drawing can be helpful. Some of the facts take on a monster-like quality, exaggerated into nightmare. Once again, drawing the monster can reduce its power a little, bringing the daylight to dawn on the phantoms of the night. All these are ways by which people can enable the different parts of their minds and hearts to talk to each other. If decisions are taken, passionately or obstinately, by just one part of ourselves, ignoring the voice of opposition within, then there might well be real difficulties later. That voice which was silenced will make itself heard, often with anger and bitterness. As far as possible, the divided self needs to be reconciled, so that the decision is taken with the consent, as it were, of all parties. The ostrich needs to be encouraged out of its hole.

I say, 'encouraged', not 'forced'. There is no point, indeed there is much harm, in trying to force the issue. Sometimes, as with Anna, there is no possibility of dialogue. She could not, would not, even consider the alternatives seriously. One can only respect that, and be ready to be around later, nonjudgementally, in case she needs to talk after the event. Listen attentively to someone, to the voice of their fears, hopes and longings, as well as to the voice of their reason; then you can sometimes find ways of expressing the counter-arguments, the 'other side', in words which they can hear.

'Facts' are endlessly tricky things. They are coloured by everyone's beliefs and emotions. Like every friend, every counsellor, I have to be constantly careful that I am not reading my own preferences and beliefs into what people say to me, and in what I reflect back to them. It is fatally easy for the sympathetic friend heavily to influence the decision being taken. Of course, we all have opinions and beliefs which are found to colour what we say. The important thing is to be aware of that, and to try not to let it limit our friend's freedom to follow her own thoughts through. Such influence is a temptation hard to resist when our deepest beliefs are involved, as they so often are in questions of divorce or abortion.

That, of course, is where humility comes in. The humility which recognises that I, like each of us, have come to my own beliefs by a path which I alone have trodden. I needed to come on that long, winding path – a path which I am still travelling. I needed to make those 'mistakes', to go down those apparent side-turnings. And other people also need to follow their own path. I cannot force them onto mine. Jesus could not, did not wish to, force the rich young man to sell up and follow him. This is an incredibly difficult lesson for most of us to learn; I certainly find it so.

Indeed, one of the hardest things in the world is to watch people close to us make what we believe to be mistakes. It seems helpful to guide their thinking, to help them out of their terrible state of indecision. But to be dominated or obviously influenced from outside in making one of these life-changing decisions is potentially to set up a source of bitterness and guilt in later years. It is no way out for your friend to be taken out of the cage of 'impossible decision' and put into the cage of 'evaded responsibility'. The bars may not be obvious at once, but they may become devastatingly clear later.

5 ‖ An uncomprehending world

'I scream but no one hears me, no one hears my screams of pain.'

'Human kind cannot bear very much reality', says the poet T.S. Eliot, leaving us to interpret him as we will. But what are these realities which are so hard to live with?

One of them is, I think, the mismatch between our deepest intuitions or beliefs about the way the world 'is', or 'should be', and the facts of experience which run, agonisingly, against those beliefs. We believe in love and justice – yet the world is hideously unloving and unjust. And allied closely to this there is a mismatch between our own picture of ourselves – which we may never have put into words consciously but which is nevertheless basic to the way we live our lives – and the very different picture which crises can sometimes force upon us. It can be a far stronger image; but this kind of very fundamental challenge can be extraordinarily difficult to handle.

Tina encountered reality in this way and it was a desperately lonely, confusing experience. For her family and friends, on the whole, either could not or would not enter into the magnitude of the struggle through which she was passing. They could see the outside facts of the case; could understand that, yes, it was bound to be a painful decision for her. But they could not comprehend just how this question of whether or not to abort affected both Tina's understanding of herself and her sense of trust in a comprehensible world – a world in which right and wrong, love and justice, had meaning and provided basic ground-rules of action.

If you love you do not kill; but Tina, *because* she loved, had to kill. If you love, you yearn to hold, to nurture, to give; Tina had to destroy her own opportunity of telling her love, showing her love, pouring out her love. She was a mother, a loving person, a matter-of-fact person who took the rough with the smooth and did not run away from stress and responsibility, so she had to deny her very self. She had to do so because of her love, her sense of responsibility, her courage; but that was hard for her to understand. It would take time. In the crisis time of decision, all that Tina could see was fragmentation, the falling apart of all the known landmarks of her self and the world around her. And she was alone with that fragmentation.

She was very alone since for her family the question of the abortion was very clear cut: painful; far from easy; but unquestionably the right thing. For her parents as well as for her husband, Joe, questioning that rightness or asking what the implications of it were for Jamie was simply unhelpful, making life harder for Tina and Joe, not easier. With many families, the assumption goes the other way: abortion is wrong, evil, a sin; there is no room for discussing the implications of the birth for the rest of the family and for the mother herself. Neither straightforward and unquestioning point of view does justice to the complex of responsibilities and circumstances through which we have to pick our way.

As I have said, it can be hard to restrain our own beliefs or assumptions from trying to indicate a friend's choice. In issues of life and death, like abortion or legalised euthanasia, this is above all difficult. Many of us have passionately held beliefs, whether moral or theological. Either we believe that abortion is the killing of a human being, never to be countenanced, or else that the foetus, in the early months, is no more 'human' than an unfertilised ovum, and that the rights of the mother are paramount. If we hold strong beliefs, then we may also think that it is right, and therefore helpful, to speak to our friends of them, in an attempt to persuade them of their validity. After all, if Tina had only been convinced that it would be *wrong* to subject herself and the family to the strains of another handicapped child, then, in theory, her decision would be very much easier: there would not really be a decision to take. It would be clear cut.

The only difficulty with that is that such 'beliefs' simply did not speak to Tina. They did not match up with the agonised questions which her heart and mind were posing – almost against her will. It was not that she *wanted* to make life complicated for herself, that she was wilfully making a big crisis out of a painful but clear situation. It was that she was having to confront, inescapably, the fact of complexity: the fact that life was messier and more complicated than her assumptions had allowed for. There was just too much reality around – and Tina was not the sort who took a sleeping tablet and closed her eyes.

I remember talking with a young mother of a nine-month-old child. It was the only such conversation I had with Linda: long and intense, springing up out of the blue over a cup of coffee one morning. Her dilemma was over whether to return to work. She loved her little daughter and was a good, caring mother. But increasingly, she was finding that being at home all day, purely as a mother, mixing with other young mothers whose primary topic of conversation was their children was becoming a prison. She was intelligent and active, not so much ambitious for promotion as needing to use her brain and creativity in a situation other than motherhood; needing the stimulation of other people whose interests paralleled her own and who would challenge her. She was noticing herself becoming irritable with baby Jackie, putting less energy into devising activities for the child. She believed that if she returned to work part time, Jackie would benefit by her mother's increased happiness; that she herself would regain her active delight and interest in the child.

But Linda's parents and friends were shocked. It was too early; she would damage the child and her own relationship with the child, would be ducking out of the responsibility she had taken on by having the baby . . . All very fine theories but they ignored the fact that love and responsibility can be shown in very varied, even contradictory, ways. We assume we know how our obligations work out in practice. But sometimes – crunch! it just does not work and we have to look again, redefine our picture of ourselves and the boundaries which we set ourselves.

Not long after our conversation Linda did follow her own leanings and go back to work. Events proved her instinct right. She was a better mother then than she had been in those increasingly arid weeks leading up to her decision. But it was a hard decision to take. Linda was extraordinarily alone in those weeks. She and her partner had recently moved so the only friends she had around were those she had made in prenatal sessions and various mothers' groups. No one shared her gnawing boredom. No one could understand her growing dread of not being able to cope with this dissatisfaction, of slipping from being a good mother to being indifferent and even coming to resent the existence of little Jackie. It was a huge anxiety for her. But to her friends and family such fears had no existence; there were simply facts which she was refusing to face about the implications and duties of motherhood. She was alone with her unhappiness and it threatened to drive her into the kind of depression or anxiety which itself acts as a wall between self and others, holding us in a world cut off from theirs.

This conflict between perceptions of the real and the unreal, the inability of others to understand what we see as the emotional and religious dimensions of the decisions we are taking, can be very difficult also in our relations with any authorities involved. As I have said, this was true in my and Karen's struggle to keep her children out of care. For Tina, loneliness in relation to her family was compounded by the medics' incomprehension of many of the roots of her distress. This is not a criticism of either doctors or nurses, though I think Tina was singularly unlucky in the nursing staff who cared for her during the abortion itself. It is difficult not to apply standard words of comfort to those going into an operation, even an abortion, when it is so routine a part of the day's work. The nurses could not enter with her into the rights and wrongs of the decision; it was not their job to do so and they probably had no time to listen to her terrors about what would be done to the foetus, to Jamie. She felt powerless to try to voice thoughts which were so out of place in the environment of busy doctors and nurses – specialists, authority figures. So she was left simply not knowing what would happen to the aborted foetus. She was unsupported in her attempts to cope with her imaginings and their implications for herself and the baby.

Priests or ministers, or friends whose religious beliefs are known and respected, can also be authority figures to us when we are in crisis. This can be a source of great strength or of damage. When people are in pain they can embrace with joy and enormous relief the comfort and certainty of religious belief. But that faith can be felt as a false sense of certainty, one which crumbles later, when the inconvenient questions born of painful experience start thrusting up through them like plants beneath cracking concrete. Or speaking of God to people in grief can work in the other direction, alienating people from a faith which seems blind and deaf to the reality of human pain. Belief can seem meaningless – painfully so – if our feelings do not match the picture of life within which it works. To say that Jamie would be safe in the loving hands of God or that he did not really exist – was merely a foetus – could not have touched Tina. For her the unborn Jamie, but not the living God, had a vivid reality. Our strongest, most lasting and influential beliefs grow from within us; we hardly know how – they are born of our experience and our own reactions to it. Such beliefs are different in kind from those which live merely in our intellects, disconnected from our emotional and spiritual responses to the world. In particular, the sense of justice, or of fairness, is deeply engrained within most of us. It is hard to accept blows which come at us against all reason, all justice: 'Why me? Why him? What have we done to deserve it?' The depth of Tina's grief for Jamie, unshared by her family and friends, made these hard questions for her to handle. She had to work out what was real to her, what did make sense out of all this confusing, conflicting medley of experience. It took time.

Tina had to reconcile her own sense of an essential fairness, a basic goodness in life, with the cruelty of the choice which she had to make. She did not have a formulated religious belief: her experience of suffering and of injustice did not coincide with a specific faith in a loving God. For religious believers the task of working out the practical implications of their faith can be extraordinarily difficult and painful – especially when their beliefs lead them in a direction different from that of those they love, trust and respect. For over a year I saw and talked regularly with a couple, both of them deeply committed Christians. She, Christina, was also a member of the Green party and an activist on environmental issues. This was not a fringe interest for her: she saw it as integral to her religious faith and vital for the future of the planet and all its living species, including humanity.

Her husband Rick did not share her belief. On the contrary, he believed that it was not the task of Christians to prescribe solutions to problems of environmental degradation or human suffering: it was their part to identify and bear witness to evil, but their witness was diluted in his eyes by endeavours to 'tell the experts what to do'.

As time passed, the convictions of both partners about the implications of their Christian faith and the lifestyles which they were called to live became increasingly disparate. Sometimes they could distance themselves from the conflict sufficiently to see the humour in it: as on the occasion when they told me of the Battle of the Washing-up Liquid. Rick – and I am not sure whether it was deliberately or not – had done the grocery shopping one week and had come home with Fairy Liquid, ignoring Christina's established habit of buying an ecologically friendly alternative. Going to use it in his absence she first swore then burst into helpless tears and then picked herself up and went storming out of the house to buy some Ecover. Neither alluded to the matter. But for over a week, until in fact they next came to see me, those two bottles of washing-up liquid stood uneasily side by side, like representatives of opposing armies, bearing witness to the conflict between Rick and Christina.

This story did not come out initially as a funny one. Christina alluded to it, her face tight, not looking at him. It represented so much for both of them, so much about the depth of their lack of communication, that they could not even talk about so apparently trivial an issue as brands of washing-up liquid. Only later – a few months later – when they were far more able to voice their differences, did the two militant plastic bottles, standing sentinel beside the hot tap, suddenly appear ludicrous. Christina and then, with more difficulty, Rick were able to begin to snort with laughter over it.

I encourage such laughter to break the tension which can twang like taut wire between couples facing crises in their personal relationships. They need its release. It is funny and at the same time far from funny. The two rival bottles represented the incompatibility of Rick's and Christina's commitments. And yet those different commitments were based in the Christian faith which they shared strongly. That faith was part of who they were, both as individuals and as a couple.

What made the dilemma sharpest for these two was the nature of the marriage vow. Christina had sworn to obey Rick. To him, her insistence on active involvement in the Green movement represented a breach of that vow made to God in the marriage service. From this standpoint he could not, would not, shift. Christina was caught in an intolerable dilemma. Either she disobeyed Rick, thus breaking an oath which she accepted unquestioningly when she was married, or she denied her deepest convictions about the implications of her faith and about the future of the world and all humanity. Once again it was an extraordinarily lonely place to be. Her friends were drawn from her church and campaigning circles; both groups were strongly committed, either to the sanctity of liturgy and Bible or to the urgency and centrality of environmental concerns. Neither could hear the validity of the other's case; Christina could hear both. She believed in both and the conflict between them put her in a mad world where she could not avoid betraying herself and her God. She was on her own – abandoned, as she often felt, even by God.

Rick would accept no need for mediation. For him the issue was clear cut, the marriage vow holding no possible alternative interpretation to that of simple obedience in all things. Christina, though, desperately needed someone with whom she could talk about this impossible dilemma – someone who would not belittle either side of the debate. Someone who, respecting both sides, would yet help her seek some sideways move which would somehow bring the two into adequate alignment. At that stage at least it was not helpful for her to hear the straightforward judgement of some of her friends: that the marriage was becoming increasingly unworkable, the paths on which the two found themselves being ever more divergent. She could not hear such arguments. Divorce was not to her at that time a realistic possibility.

And it is important, in such a situation, not to try to force simplistic solutions upon our friends. Whatever our own beliefs we have somehow to try to inhabit their world, seeing through the spectacles of their beliefs and finding words and ways forward which begin at that point, having meaning to our friends where they are. We human beings cannot suddenly adopt radically new beliefs: we have to arrive at them in our own time, travelling forward from and through our own experience. As their friends we may – indeed almost certainly will – have hopes about the beliefs and actions towards which they may move. But if they are ever to be whole people, at ease with themselves, they need to find their own way. They need to be supported by our love and our endeavours to understand them imaginatively, probably challenged by our alternative points of view but not to be the subject of dictation. That can only compound the confusion and loneliness – or give a false sense of security which may collapse at any point.

Often and often, people with whom I have worked have needed to be angry with 'the fates', or with God, whichever form their beliefs take. Again this can be one of the hardest experiences for a committed believer. An enormous guilt and anxiety is entwined with anger – above all anger against those whom we ought to love, to revere, to be thankful to; above all, then, against our parents and God, precisely those with whom often we most need to be angry. I am not suggesting by that that our parents have necessarily done terrible things to us which 'deserve' a powerful response, though in many cases, in the most respectable families, one or other parent has indeed abused the child in any of a multitude of ways. But the taboo against anger with parents is commonly so strong that we have all our lives been unable to feel or express it when we have felt such anger, whatever the cause which has provoked it. Fermenting away inside us, unexpressed and unacknowledged, this kind of strong emotion can fertilize a basic sense of unease with the world: the sense of being in some sense disconnected from others; our real selves invisible, alone and quite probably laden with a scarcely formulated sense of guilt.

Anger with God runs parallel with this anger with parents. Both can help to cut religious believers off from their own spiritual communities. Such emotions often simply do not fit with the theology which many believers profess. They are seen as signs of the failure of faith, as an inability either to understand the will of God for us in this situation or to trust that the whole terrible tangle will ultimately lead to good. Hand in hand with those guilts often comes fear. Consciously or unconsciously, perhaps a legacy of our childhoods, the image which many of us carry is of a stern and all-powerful Deity: majestic, royal, unapproachable.

Anger with such a being seems blasphemous. We fear the retaliatory anger of this medieval potentate which is our image of God. Perhaps though, it is not an image of God but an idol, created in a shape born of our human experiences; an idol from which we need to be freed.

It is probably never possible to be entirely free of such distorting images of God. But it can be good to become aware of them, perhaps to seek out their sources in our own pasts and to let the love and forgiveness and acceptance of God seep past and through them. My own image of God as authority figure, distant and fearsome, was revolutionised when I first read the *Don Camillo* books some thirty years ago. Here was a God it was possible to talk to, to argue with and to reproach when things went unfairly wrong, with whom one could have jokes, yet who was the source of guidance and strength through it all.

Undoubtedly, Christina felt at times a savage anger with the God who had led her into this inescapable, bleak cul-de-sac, presenting her with incompatible commandments which she could never fulfil, struggle as she would. That was a response which she had never been able to confess either to Rick or to her fellow church members. I think it would have been hard for her also to confess it to her friends within the Green party, out of a deep-rooted instinct of loyalty to her own faith. She had been able to talk of it to me to some extent, since I am unconnected with either group. It was a genuine release to be able to voice it and to have it received nonjudgementally: to realise that I saw it as a reaction which was not only natural and perhaps inevitable but was actually valid.

There are times, I think, when if believers are not angry with God they are denying the powers of thought and emotion which they believe to be God-given. Job, after all, was commended by God for his questioning, respected by God as a man of integrity and honesty even though his power to judge God was fiercely questioned by the deity. To deny such responses of anger to the cruelties of life can mean a refusal to acknowledge their reality, thus cutting ourselves off from the pain of our fellow human beings. So we come to bustle past the wounded traveller, telling ourselves that her hurt cannot be as bad as it looks: a good God would not allow it. Or if God had intended it, then it must be for a good purpose, enabling us to pray a quick 'thy will be done' and hurry on our way. Thus to deny the ways in which the loving purposes of God do crash against the reality of human pain can set up a deep, if hidden, contradiction within us. It emerges when we come up against griefs which cannot be ignored or belittled.

So it seems to me helpful not to put thoughts or words into our friends' mouths, but to help them acknowledge and give voice to such feelings of anger if that is indeed what is fermenting inside them. Listening nonjudgementally so that they are not left in the lonely terror of feeling emotions which they believe to be wrong, sinful, even evil. Hearing also the bewilderment and fear of an identity under threat: 'Why isn't my faith strong enough to bear this? I thought I believed in the one who said that no cross would be too heavy to bear'. For many Christians there is a strongly rooted belief that our faith should enable us to accept whatever God sends. And when we find difficulty in accepting, when we are outraged by the injustices done to ourselves or to others, then it is indeed hard to avoid a sense of guilt and failure. There is a feeling of being an outcast, no longer worthy to be one of the community of faith; a sense, perhaps, of being punished for some unknown fault.

It can be very helpful to express such thoughts in writing or painting, as a way of acknowledging to ourselves the hitherto unspeakable angers and confusions which we are experiencing. Talking about them can be even better, in order to break the isolation into which they thrust us. Best of all, we need a friend who can hear what we have to say without condemning us – a friend, ideally, who shares that faith and whose integrity we respect. Facile words of comfort, which refuse to take seriously either the strength of feeling being expressed, or its implications for the underlying faith, are not helpful. Both our anger and the corresponding confusion, fear and guilt need to be heard. Being a listening ear for our friends we are unlikely to be able to produce any 'solutions' to the collisions between a loving God and the fact of suffering and injustice. But we can mitigate the loneliness and despair which so often go along with that struggle.

Christina felt anger with the God who presented her, as she felt, with two mutually contradictory sets of injunctions: to obey her husband and to obey the promptings which drove her to political action. Hers was an extraordinarily painful dilemma – the more so as the person with whom she was accustomed to join in prayer and discussion over problems was the person to whom the issue was clear cut: her husband himself.

I worked with another family, this time committed Muslims, who faced a very different yet comparable tension of faith. I know very little of Islam, though I have respected very highly the commitment and integrity of those Muslims with whom I have come into contact. Often I have found that acceptance of the will of God, of Allah, is central to their understanding of faith.

This family had had a run of extraordinary bad fortune. Farid, the father, was a tailor, whose job with a firm making cheap clothing had ended. They had bought their council house then interest rates shot up, bringing the threat of repossession by the building society daily closer. Finally their youngest child had been diagnosed as having incurable cancer. It was this which finished Farid. The mother, despite her grief, came to accept the inevitability of her daughter's death. So did the child who told her mother in the end that she was looking forward to her own release. Farid could not accept it: struggling with his own understanding of faith, struggling with an anger against God which he could not admit, it was a truly terrible time for him. In the face of the doctors' opinions he was committed to struggle for his daughter's life, to the extent of trying to arrange to take her to China where he had heard of miracle cancer cures. On the evening of the day when he was told that she would not survive the flight, she died.

As a woman and a non-Muslim, I was not the right person to be able to help Farid. But that experience did highlight for me once again the importance of trying to understand, at least in outline, the shape of our friends' beliefs, in order that we can hear and respect the nature of the struggle through which they are going in taking the decisions they have to take. With those friends with other cultures or beliefs this can be difficult. It is, though, a challenge which is deeply enriching for us as we learn more of the incredible variety of approaches to life and belief.

And amongst that richness I have to confess that I find extraordinarily refreshing the forthright attitude of one Catholic family with whom I worked over a good many years. As yet another disaster struck – the mother's hours being cut at work or the children's football going through next door's picture window – Mrs Arthur would sniff. 'Not trying hard enough, He isn't. Time He gave us a break'. And so, I am sure, she told Him. Her God was one who struggled with her in the messiness of everyday life, with its unscheduled disasters and unexpected delights – a suffering, vulnerable, understanding God. She also had at least one good friend to whom she could go in rage or despair or bafflement and who knew enough of her situation and beliefs to hear her, accept her, and at times challenge her in a way which she could hear and respect. They were a good pair: if either had to go to the doctor or to Social Services, they would often go together, giving each other courage to voice the questions and doubts which otherwise would have haunted them as Tina's haunted her. Such friends are good to have.

6 | *The decision*

'I love you so much that I must let you go.'

Loving one another creates very complicated – and peculiar – power relationships. My love for my children gives them an immense power to hurt and manipulate me, and vice versa. And their love for me gives me a huge responsibility towards them; particularly when they were small, it gave me both power over and responsibility to them. As children, they trusted and depended upon their father and me. In making decisions about where to live, about my husband accepting a job which would send him abroad a lot, about whether as a result to send the children to boarding school, about my elderly mother coming to live with us in our small house, we were making choices on behalf of our children, which would dramatically affect the way in which they grew up. This was, in a factual way, our legal responsibility to the children we had brought into the world.

But it was more than that: the fact that there was love between the children and us made it far more. Because of that bond of love and dependency – a two-way dependency, for parents are, in different ways, heavily dependent upon their own children – the choices we made *represented* very important things for our children. Through the choices we make, our children deduce things about the love we have for them. The conclusions they come to are based on a whole medley of fact and semi-fantasy: we can all remember minute incidents in our childhood which, for us, contained powerful messages about our relationship with our parents, incidents of which our poor parents were probably blissfully oblivious. But there it is: where we love one another we have power over one another, for better or worse. The important thing is to recognise that uncomfortable fact, and then to accept it – with a certain humour. We can only do our best, and the more we agonise about it all, the more we are likely to cause our children to agonise.

So, because we love and are loved, we have power; and this love drives us at times to take remarkably ruthless decisions. Tina is one of the most courageous and honest people of my acquaintance, for the clarity with which she faced the nature of the decision she was taking. She had no illusions about the ruthlessness which she was having to use. Tina had her child aborted because she loved him; because she could not bear him to be born into a world of incomprehensible suffering; nor could she bear her own responsibility for giving him so imperfect a future. It was a decision taken on behalf of a person who could never speak for himself, in the face of future possibilities which could never be known. It was a decision taken also on behalf of her three small daughters, none of them of an age to take shared responsibility in it, yet on whose lives a severely handicapped small brother would have such an impact. Her choice was made together with Joe, who never had any doubts about it; but, in the final analysis, the power of life and death was Tina's. Knowing all this, Tina made her choice. It is an awesome responsibility for any person; the fact that she made this decision precisely *because* she loved Jamie so much makes the full acknowledgement of responsibility at once more painful and, curiously, more possible.

Of course, the issue at stake is not always so life-and-death. A little while ago, I remember talking with a woman whose husband's job had been moved from Surrey to Birmingham. The children were in the middle of the school courses; both sets of grandparents were in the south-east of England. They had had to decide between uprooting their children at just the wrong moment, or running the very real risk of long-term unemployment. They had decided to stay in Surrey. Again and again as we talked – we both had to spend a few days in hospital, so there was plenty of time! – Mrs Webb would say, 'We thought we were doing the right thing. It was so difficult. It'll be so hard if their dad's out of work for long. But we thought it was the right thing.' She told me of the nearly sleepless nights between taking the decision and finally writing the letter of resignation to the firm. It was a hard time.

There is, of course, no 'right' decision in this situation. The Webbs, and Tina, could with equal integrity and good sense have made the opposite choice. Faced with the probability or the fact of a handicapped baby, some parents I have known have refused abortion, fostering or adoption, believing that their love for this child will, must, overcome all the difficulties and costs involved in bringing her or him up. Karen, of the twenty-four stone and intermittent prostitution, refused, through all the painful turmoil of her long medical treatment, and even as her death came manifestly nearer, to allow her three children to be fostered.

Karen's was one of the dirtiest houses I have ever been in, and her parenting did not conform to any known textbook. Social Services were called in following neighbours' complaints about rats; I would often call in the middle of the day to find Karen recumbent in her front room, still in her night clothes, the chaos and filth accumulated around her. The children were no less dirty, their few clothes rarely – and sketchily – washed. They, and Karen's permanent partner, accepted the occasional presence of her various clients: she, after all, worked for her living.

Yet the children were always well nourished, Karen having learnt from her partner and clients the West Indian art of cooking good meals on a small budget. She would take the children to and from school, and was always well stocked with proud stories of their progress there, or with colourfully abusive accounts of any criticism by teachers or neighbours. The energy which she put into the happiness of her children was quite phenomenal, against all the odds. I remember her small daughter hurtling indoors one day as I sat talking with Karen, demanding to be shown how to cross her arms across her chest while skipping. Instantly and entirely engrossed in this question, Karen headed out into the minute and rubbish-filled back garden, there to demonstrate the technique, only to find a technical hitch in mid-skip – her arms would no longer cross around her front. My memory of Karen, helplessly collapsed with laughter in that scruffy little garden, matches my memory of Karen when we went together to the fun fair, shaking with mirth as two men tried to extract her from the dodgem into which she had enthusiastically wedged herself at the urgent entreaty of her offspring. If those children did not have a happy childhood, it was not for want of trying on their mother's part.

As Karen's health deteriorated, and the end came in sight, a real dilemma presented itself to the Social Services. Karen fought like a tiger. She loved those children; they loved and trusted her deeply and uncritically. It was a classic problem: whether they should stay where they were loved, yet where the amenities of life were so markedly lacking; or go to foster parents or a home, where there would be no rats – and no comparable love either. Be the cost to her what it may – and it was very considerable as she weakened – Karen was clear about her decision. For the statutory authorities, the question was a desperately difficult one, their responsibilities hard to resolve. They were won over by Karen's genuineness, and the children stayed at home.

Karen was neither as intelligent nor as self-aware as Tina. She did not spell out for herself the extent and nature of her responsibility to those children, yet she was well aware that whichever decision she took and persuaded the authorities to take, it would have vital implications for the children. We talked about it together and discussed the costs; Karen knew them well.

Thinking about Tina and Karen, and about their experience of responsibility and guilt, I am reminded of my own parallel experience – the time when I too had to take responsibility, whatever I did, for hurting and probably damaging someone I love, the time when my daughter became severely anorexic. It was a complicated, muddled, incredibly tense and overwrought time. But one decision was very clear: her father and I had to decide, each of us for ourselves, whether to challenge our daughter's fantasies, the web of desperate fears with which she had surrounded herself and which was expressed and also reinforced by her refusal to eat; or whether to be supportive, accepting of her vision of the world and her place in it. If we challenged, then we risked driving her further into that fog of desperate fear; by shattering her trust in us, we might possibly break also her last contact with the outer world's reality. If we accepted, we were colluding in her fantasy, possibly confirming her in it, possibly denying her a more profound *need* to be challenged and contained by those she trusted. We had no one clear-cut moment of decision – no more than Tina or Karen did. But from day to day and night to night we were making that decision; and, at times, we were brought up short by one of those moments of clarity about our responsibility.

As with Tina and Karen, it was not a question of whether we loved, but of how that love should be expressed. The hell of it was that our love could, with equal logic, pull us in either of the two diametrically opposed directions. In that kind of situation, where all kinds of emotional manipulation, semi-conscious and unconscious, is going on, one can have very little doubt about the power which love does give us over each other. Our daughter exerted enormous power over her family; likewise, we had more influence, for good or ill, over her than did anyone else. That is the way it is – but it is uncomfortable to recognise it.

I am not suggesting that it is 'right', or constructive, to spend acres of time agonising over 'the reality of my responsibility'. Not at all. I am merely saying that many of us *do*, as a matter of experience, come to such paralysing moments of awareness – quite probably more than once; and that those moments are extraordinarily painful in their clarity. Yet I am also suggesting that for many of us it is helpful to pass through such moments: it is honest, and wholeness can best be built upon honesty.

For there is a distinction between accepting responsibility and being tied up in knots by guilt. Or, to put it differently, a distinction between a legalistic guilt, which is – primarily – a matter of fact and rational judgement, and neurotic guilt, which cleaves to, cannot let go of, that legalistic fact of responsibility, allowing our whole picture of ourselves and the world to become dominated by it. It is a vital distinction; and clearly recognising the actual responsibility can be a useful tool in avoiding the bugbear guilt.

How? Many people have found by experience that if they deny certain things about themselves, certain memories or responsibilities, these things return to plague them later. We may cover memories in many layers, tie them up and put them in the attic; but at some level, we remain aware that they are there. Their shrouded forms lurk in the corners of our mind, becoming increasingly misshapen and horrible to our imagination. We may very well not know what it is that is troubling us, but *something* is affecting our ability to think and feel clearly on other – apparently unrelated – matters. And, quite probably, we build up layers of fantasy about ourselves, to help cover over that original memory, until we run into danger of forgetting who we originally were. That way lies real confusion and unhappiness.

So, when we are being driven by circumstances to take ruthless decisions for and about others – and it is particularly difficult about those we love – it is good if we are able to be ruthless with ourselves also, in recognising this fact of responsibility. It is a fact then, hard and unyielding, deeply painful; but with a shape and size which can be seen and, in a sense, accepted. Since its size can be seen, so can the limits of that size. Far better, this, than letting it become a monster which dominates our lives.

It would be too clear cut to suggest that if we do not recognise our responsibility, then we will be tied up with guilt; or the reverse – that if we do recognise the legalistic responsibility, then the monster Guilt will not plague us. I am certainly far from free from guilts of all sorts, as a parent, for things whose seriousness I did recognise, and for those which I did not. I am still capable, in the middle of the night, of waking up and churning over our decision to send the children to boarding school. We did think very hard about the pros and cons at the time. But, in the watches of the night, I am inclined now to think that we did not think hard enough, that we did not really envisage the implications for the children, what it would mean to them. I suppose that, with hindsight, we can always flog ourselves in this kind of way, especially when we are vulnerable, when we are tired or unwell. Nevertheless, I do think it is true to say that the potential for future grief can be made greater or smaller by our ability to be honest at the time in thinking through as many of the implications as we can see, as both Tina and Karen were.

Friends are, of course, incredibly important at such times of decision-taking. They are both a safety fuse, allowing us to explode our grief, anger and guilt, and a mirror, enabling us to see ourselves. Tina talked, a little, to me before the abortion; she talked of course to her diary – another kind of friend – and she could and did talk to a couple of close friends. I am not, by nature, a natural confider. But there was one friend in particular who knew, in outline at least, the dimensions of our daughter's problem. There was nothing she could do; nothing, really, that she could say. But I knew that she knew just how impossible was the grief and the guilt; she knew that I was floundering around, inevitably damaging the child I was so desperate to support and help. At the same time, she was able, with her brusque common sense and sense of humour, to stop me when she saw me beginning to wallow, irrationally and unconstructively, in my own guilt. But she knew the shape of the hell, and she accepted me in the thick of it. She gave me her love and, when I wanted them, her ears and a shoulder to cry on through it all. Now she is gone, I miss her badly. In that acceptance by another there is a kind of absolution. It helps us cope with those dark moments when the responsibility appears all too clearly before us.

For absolution is desperately needed at such times. There is something supremely, perhaps ineradicably egoistic about us human beings. Tina was profoundly concerned about the pain to be suffered by her son – including the pain about which she fantasised, the pain of the abandoned foetus. But she was also inescapably concerned for her own pain, for her own inability to cope with his handicap, with her own searing responsibility for what she was – either way – doing to him. She needed to act in a way which minimised that burden: though it greatly worsened the immediate horror, the abortion meant that she would not have to go through years carrying the responsibility for giving Jamie a life narrowed by sickness and disability. For my part, I could not cope with the burden of possibly pushing my daughter into the final desperation; there was a limit to how much I could handle. That is not an expression of my guiltiness – not at all; it is a statement of fact. We are only human, and we call on the resources which are available to us. We do what we can.

That is not to deny the reality of spiritual resources – that capacity for communion with something greater than ourselves which makes humanity what it is – or potentially is. There must be so many of us who, in our varied contexts, find ourselves hitting the very bottom of our strength; and who find in that total abjectness a silent strength which upholds and steadies us. Tina has talked to me in similar terms of her faith – not a faith of creeds and Sunday worship, but a silent faith born out of experience.

I have commented that what one needs at such times is absolution. In a sense, of course, there is no absolution: the responsibility for doing damage is inescapable. But there is a kind of absolution in recognising that very inescapability, and somehow finding oneself accepted within it. It is an impossible situation, and we do what we can.

That acceptance is represented by the nonjudgemental love of friends. It is also found, deep down, in that silent place where strength is.

I was not pointed to that place by anyone else; nor, I think, were Tina or Karen. Indeed, I would not have welcomed anyone's attempts to point me there: it is incredibly difficult for the most genuine, the most well-meaning words of wisdom and counsel to sound anything but hideously distant from the immediacy of our own experience and pain. These words which I am writing now will seem equally distant from those who are themselves caught in the hell of choice and guilt – as well as seeming remarkably unhelpful to any whose friends are going through it. All I can say is that, even in the darkest moments – or perhaps especially in those – it is possible to go right through the bottom of the pit, and find that in some way, the fact of responsibility for a horrible act is blended with a kind of acceptance that we did what we could. We 'meant well', if you like. In some situations, that is the best we can do – and it is not easily done. Such a sense of acceptance does not necessarily last; but it is a discovery, made through the loving companionship of friends, or through times of worship, which gives us enough strength to carry on trying.

Not all of us, of course, have this experience of recognising what we are doing to one another by our decisions and actions. None of us come to such traumas from the same place; what we bring to them, out of our experience of the past, is very different: we are vulnerable and strong in different places, and to different degrees. So our ability to take on board the implications of our choices – and the desirability for us of realising it – is very variable. Many men who have fought in war shrug their experience off, belittling its significance. Some of those, I believe, would do better – for themselves and, perhaps even more importantly, for both their families and the societies in which they live – to acknowledge with more honesty the magnitude of the events through which they have lived. But for others, particularly the enlisted, involuntary soldiers, such an acknowledgement could be more than they could bear. There are some people for whom some shadows are too powerful. And, of course, those same people frequently have strengths which others lack. It is not a case of 'the strong and the weak', merely of our being different.

I remember very clearly one couple's response to the birth of a slightly brain-damaged child. They already had three children, all boys; the fourth was also a boy. Martin, the father, firmly believed that whatever the cost to parents and siblings, the baby was a part of the family, already loved and valued as a person, and they should keep him. He was an immensely resilient, loving man, who already did much of the parenting for the three boys. His wife, Clare, reacted entirely differently. Clare was from the first unable to handle the new child; she was repelled by the idea of handicap, hardly able to see or hold him. She was insistent that the baby must go for adoption. For her, there was no choice; the cost to the other boys and to the marriage would be far too great. Unless the baby went, she would – and would take her three elder sons with her. By taking her stand on the impossibility of keeping the baby, Clare simply denied her own responsibility for the decision. It was not, to her eyes, in her own hands. A similar evasion of responsibility is very commonly taken by those who take refuge in the doctor or social worker as the repository of all wisdom: 'It is their decision, not mine.'

I do not, cannot, blame Clare. I, and others, challenged her belief – challenged it very hard, in various ways. But she held to it, and I came to accept that she was acting out of her own necessity. The particular shape of Clare's vulnerability made hers a very different decision from that which Tina had to face; Clare could not let herself love this baby, she could not let herself acknowledge that it played any part in the family's life, in the life of his brothers. Clare denied both pain and responsibility, thereby taking on, albeit unconsciously, a very grave responsibility for affecting – even manipulating – the emotions and lives of her family. Hers was a necessity which conflicted directly with that of her husband. The choice which he had to make was a desperately difficult one – to accept her choice, or to split the family. He chose the former.

In many ways Clare is, now, a far less free person than Tina. I do not know to what extent the events and passions of those weeks recur consciously to her mind. But she never experienced what the dramatists call catharisis: the fine-strung moment when all the emotions are gathered together to a point of decision, recognition and acceptance. This is the moment which Tina reflected when she wrote, 'I loved him so much that I had to let him go.' In reality, it is rarely so tidy and clear cut. But such honesty, however confusedly achieved, can have a cleansing effect.

And afterwards, life goes on – human beings are so incredibly resilient. I'd never have believed that I could possibly laugh at anything to do with that period of anorexia. And nor would it have been helpful if anyone had told me at the time that we would 'come through it' or 'get over it'. At the time, we could not believe in the possibility of any light at the end of the tunnel. But we – my husband, daughter and I – have now laughed, ruefully, at times almost hysterically, at some of the wild insanities of that time. And my daughter has, similarly, talked and laughed with her brothers and sister.

We have been, in greater and lesser ways, changed by our experiences – one is not the same at the end of them as one would have been. And the fact of responsibility remains there in the memory, and returns sometimes. Nevertheless, we have let go of much of the trauma of that time – after all, it is a long time ago now. Tina and Joe, too, have laughed, tenderly and wryly, at some of their memories surrounding Jamie. As for Karen, laughter was never far away at any time. She had an inimitable detachment: at one moment, the bitterest tragedy; the next, her eye would catch mine, her mouth would twitch . . . . I cannot claim that resilience for myself – but I have loved and admired it in Karen and in others.

7 || *The unbearableness of decision*

'Let me go home.'

How many of us know the nightmare situation when, having made a choice after careful thought, we find ourselves suddenly or gradually convinced that it was a wrong decision? Absolutely certain that it is necessary to backtrack – fast – before it is too late. Or, alternatively, unable any longer to bear the implications of the decision: terrified and torn with grief at the idea of what we have taken on.

And how many of us have been in the position of sitting with a friend, one with whom we have talked through long hours of decision-taking, hearing her or him coming out – hysterically or with frightening calm – with this rejection of their choice? How does the person in this position discern whether her change of heart is well founded, or whether it is merely a panic or revulsion which was perhaps almost inevitable, but which will pass. And how does the friend help her to judge?

Few major decisions are taken and implemented straightaway. For most of us, there is the terrible time of waiting between the decision and the moment when it is done, when it becomes irrevocable. It is hard to keep heart and mind nerved for the hideous act in the interim. So hard that, in the event, many of us cannot take the decision. Our minds waver, torn between the possibilities open to us, until events take control and, one way or another, the thing decides itself.

This last-ditch wavering takes two, very different, forms. There is the essentially irrational response, the panic or grief which drives us to say, 'No, no – let me out!' Or there is the eleventh-hour rethink, which somehow sees the problem from a different perspective, involving perhaps a different slant on the implications, for self or for the others involved. Tina was in the former state, as she lay on her hospital bed. Grief at what she was doing was pretty well more than she could bear.

Tina thought out her choice long and agonisedly. Acknowledging to the full her own longing for this baby, little Jamie, she persuaded herself that for his sake as well as for Joe and the other children, and ultimately for her own sake, this thing had to be. She did not change her mind – not until she was lying on the hospital bed, waiting to go into surgery. Not that she had a sudden blinding inspiration that this was the wrong thing, that she had to dress and flee. Only, I think, that she suddenly longed, with all her heart and soul, for someone to say to her, 'You don't want this. Come on, dress; go. It's all right for you to go.' Tina was mourning the loss of her baby well before that abortion took place – inevitably so. And now, her longing to go home was in part the longing of every bereaved person, to be told that it has not really happened, that it has all been a bad dream. Go home, wake up, it is all right, the burden has gone.

I have known a similar situation myself when, locked into a course of action by my own previous decision, I have been wracked by the longing for someone to set me free, to break the momentum in which I am caught. It is a hideous sense of paralysis, of powerlessness, of near panic which has to be caught and contained before it escapes from all rational control.

On other occasions I have made a decision, having – as I thought – worked through all the pros and cons. Then, at the eleventh hour, I have become quite convinced of my mistake. I *know* that I have chosen wrongly – know it as firmly as, just before, I had been convinced that this was the best decision I could make. This decision, like the former one, is fully rational, based on good solid grounds. Only it takes different things into consideration, ranks them differently, sets different priorities. I end up in limbo, not knowing which way to jump. What grounds are there for judging, when one's certainties can so shift?

Joe handled Tina's moment of change of heart as well as he could do in the circumstances: not letting it sway his own sense of conviction that they had to go on with the abortion. He acted instinctively, for he himself had no doubts about the matter, had never had doubts. But he also knew, I suspect, that his own resilience would start to give way were all the indecision to begin again. So, while Tina was longing to be told it was all right to pull out, all right to get up and leave the hospital, he gave her an equally clear message in the opposite direction: he told her that she must stay, that their decision was the right one. He took some of the burden of responsibility from her and was willing to share it himself. Indeed, he was anxious to do so, being so clear that it was right to have the abortion.

It is an immense responsibility to take, to be thus authoritative. Yet sometimes, it is just what the suffering person needs – to be told that there is no longer a choice; that the time for decision-taking is over; that the burden of responsibility has shifted to the past.

For someone like Tina, facing the sudden paralysis, the sense of being spun into the wrong future, this kind of solid rock can be just what is needed. At the least, it can carry her through the panic, prevent her from giving way to it even though she experiences no active sense of relief – even though she may resent the controlling hand; until she emerges on the far side, glad to have been held, however unwelcome it may have been at the time. But the hard part, for the friend, is judging whether this is her state of mind. There can be just a hair's breadth between thus constructively containing panic, and destructively trying to control what needs not to be controlled by outside forces.

If I can again call on my own personal experience, there were times when my daughter, having earlier agreed to join us for the evening, changed her mind at the last moment.

Sometimes, I judged it right to try to challenge and contain her fear, to attempt a tone of authority in bidding her take some food, or face our visitors. Just occasionally, it worked – almost beyond hope, it worked; and she was glad to be thus contained. She was glad not to spin off into her mind-whirling panic-fear of seeing people or of eating; glad to be channelled into a decision to come downstairs. More often, it was not successful: the attempt to contain her fear drove her further into terror, and she was confirmed in her obstinate refusal to revert to the earlier, calmer decision. Even now, I do not know how I could have distinguished one moment from the other; how I could have altered, subtly, my tone of voice to make it possible for her to hear me. Nor, incidentally, does she – for we have talked about precisely this dilemma, remembering the past. The problem for me, as for Joe, was not to work out which was the desirable course of action. I believed very firmly, and still believe, that it was good when she was able to master those terrors, and to unmask their illusory nature. Panic is rarely a better guide to action than the initial, more rational conclusion. The problem was how to throw a lifeline to my daughter that she could let herself see and grasp.

I do not think there is a way of knowing how to do this. We can only work on our knowledge of the person struggling with her decision, and our sense of her condition. To people lost in panic or in grief, I am not sure that it is ever helpful to produce rational arguments to win them back to their former acceptance of their decision. In bitter sorrow, such rationality can appear deeply – even vilely – inappropriate, a different language. In the depths of panic and fear, we cannot hear such words – again, it is another language. We do need to be held, hugged, contained. Even when being challenged, we need to be held, reassured, given the strength which comes with loving. So the skill is in finding the words which will touch and connect, and in finding the kind of physical contact which will be helpful: this can be most important of all. Between women friends, hugging is often the natural move. For men, and between men and women, it can be less easy; to hold a hand, or put an arm around the shoulders may seem the appropriate, the natural gesture. At such times, we often need to overcome our very British inhibitions against touching. Tina badly needed to be hugged and held, that day on her hospital bed. Something as simple as that would have helped.

But if the fear or grief or anger is not so intense, the brusque, apparently unsympathetic reminder of rational reality can be just what is needed. That is, effectively, what Joe gave to Tina: a simple reassertion of the original decision. For Tina, I do not think it actually gave relief. It carried her through – that is about all. For others, sometimes, it can act as the slap around the face of a hysterical person – it breaks the tension. I have done this kind of thing – with inward fear and trembling – with a young woman, Alison, just before her marriage. I had talked with her around the original decision to marry. Now, at the eleventh hour, she was overcome with panic. Was this the right decision? How could she be sure? What if either of them found the constriction, the responsibilities of marriage overwhelming? Was it not better to pull out now than to risk it, for herself and for him?

I reminded Alison, then, of the shape of her original decision to go ahead; of the things which had made it appear so manifestly the right thing. I did believe that the frame of mind in which she had made that decision, not this present panic-stricken one, was the real Alison. Had I supported her panic and said, 'Right, maybe you need more time to think it all through', the marriage would undoubtedly have been delayed. I believed that she would be giving herself, and her fiancé, a desperately confusing and bitter time of anxiety – unnecessarily. I hope that I did the right thing. For me then, as for Joe by Tina's bed, it was a very big responsibility. We act by a kind of amalgam of instinct and rational thought, responding to our knowledge of our friend and to our sense of the present moment. That's the best we can do.

Of course, there are people so chronically unable to take decisions that a friend's task can become quite hilariously unmanageable. Over many years, I was in frequent contact with a wonderful but utterly unselfconfident woman. It became increasingly clear that for her to take a decision was to ensure that by the next day she would have become entirely certain that she had made a mistake, and must act in the diametrically opposed way. I felt a bit like a dog chasing a rabbit. There I would be, thinking I had pinned her down to a decision – and there she would be, haring off another way, with me hurtling helplessly in the wrong direction. Just how, and at what point, to pounce so that she had finally to commit herself never became clear to me. It became incredibly funny. She would come in and launch into an explanation of just why it was she had changed her mind, her thin monkey-face taut and earnest; then she would catch sight of my expression, would tilt me a little sideways glance, half deprecating, half astonished, as she realised that we had been in this situation before.

It did become a bit stressful for everyone's nerves, though, when it came to the eleventh hour of her wedding. Panic at this stage is not uncommon, hardly surprisingly. It was her third marriage, and there she was, dressed up in white tulle with her two daughters and small son in frills and bow tie to attend her, when the doubts struck. I was not with her, thankfully. The combined endeavours of the family carried her as far as the church, where her anxious face peered up from beneath the veil at the clergyman. 'Do you think I'm doing the right thing?' she asked. I hope he had the skill to send her up the aisle happy. Had she been dissuaded, of course, she would have quickly gone full circle; the wedding dress would have been back in action before long.

In fact, her indecisiveness did have its tragic consequences also. Long had been the agonies before she had finally gone ahead with a separation from her previous husband. His violence had to become grotesque before she could steel herself long enough to act before she changed her mind again. She found it hard, though, to concentrate her mind even on her own family tragedy. I can see her now, sitting on her sofa with its big red floral design, crying and trembling uncontrollably as she recounted the latest horror. Then her eyes slid sideways, catching sight of the fat-faced rag doll she was making for her youngest son; unthinkingly, she picked it up and started sewing again, her tears drying forgotten on her cheeks. The doll was uncannily like its prospective owner. The whole situation felt at times like a scene from a modern farce. The awfulness was real, only, as so often, it was just a whisker from high comedy. That happens so often, that it is as well not to be surprised by it – by the way our high tragedies suddenly dissolve into wry or helpless laughter. Being human is not always particularly dignified, and that is just as well.

Weddings are the prime time for last-minute second thoughts, sometimes driven by panic, sometimes by a real reappraisal of the decision. Georgina is the daughter of friends; now, years after her marriage nearly took place, she is happily single. But it was only on the night before the wedding that the implications of what marriage entailed really hit her. I have talked about the cathartic moment when we recognise and accept responsibility for what we are doing. Well, Georgina recognised that she could *not* take responsibility for this act. She had been in love, not with her fiancé, but with the idea of being married. And now, imagining the reality of actually being married to him, of living with him permanently, having undertaken that mutual investment in one another's happiness and wellbeing. . . . Her parents told us afterwards of the unmitigated hell of that night as they talked with her, trying to discern whether this was simply stage fright or whether it was real; whether she needed more time, or whether her decision had to be presented as final; then of the next morning, as they set the wheels in motion to cancel the whole undertaking. It was an occasion when the original decision, apparently so carefully and responsibly taken, was in fact surrounded by a web of illusion and idealisation. It took the shock of the impending reality of marriage to shatter those illusions and set Georgina free to think and imagine clearly.

It can happen that, as for Georgina, starting to put a decision into action can be precisely the goad which we need to recognise that our choice was a mistaken one. For many women, adoption can seem the best path for their child, until it comes to the moment of signing the papers, when the reality of what is to be done and what it means for the future of child and mother, cuts through all the rationalisations and beliefs and makes it impossible to go on – which is, of course, unspeakably shattering for the adoptive parents, who have often fostered the child over months or years.

The same thing happens with divorce. I have been regularly in contact with a young married woman who has talked with me endlessly about her need and desire for legal separation from her husband. Increasingly, over the weeks, she had become more fixed and determined in her decision, more attached to the vision of what a return to single life might be like. Until, that is, the deeply traumatic interview at which she told him, in my presence, what she was thinking and intending. He was shattered – but then she had known he would be. I simply do not know just how it was that the vision in her mind altered. The impending reality of that single life, that separation from him, made her realise that she had been building up an illusion, that it was not what she, in her strongest self, wanted. The task changed: it was now how the two of them, together, could rebuild their marriage on a fuller and more lasting basis.

It takes courage to stop a decision once the momentum has set in. Simply to admit those last-minute doubts tends to be incredibly difficult. My young married woman friend did not actually spell out to me that she was regretting her decision. Her regret was there in her hesitant speech, in her uncertain manner, the hand smoothing her skirt, eyes glancing down, glancing at me again, and again down to that hand, so restless in her lap. It was evident in the half-heartedness with which she spoke of the next move, of the future. We talked around and around until finally I was able to lead up, gently, to the obvious question: whether she was quite certain that this was the best way forward, for herself, him and the children. And she was able to look quickly at me with an expression of uncertainty and grief which I had never previously seen in her, and say, helplessly, 'I don't know – I just don't know.'

At times people are simply unable to recant, even though they are sure they have actually made the wrong choice. There are many reasons; fear of the authorities can be a very potent one. When we are facing unfamiliar forces – magistrates, lawyers, doctors, remote and faceless Personnel Departments – anything which seems to challenge their authority, or to muck them about, can seem quite impossible. I remember very clearly one father, sitting beside the bed of his daughter, a quite delightful, loving child named Fatima. She had a rare condition, a severe curvature of the spine. The decision was whether to operate, risking her life, or to allow her to become more and more twisted – she was just curling up like a corkscrew. The decision to operate had gone ahead. She was just ten, and very intelligent. She knew about it and its implications and, like so many children, she was shatteringly courageous. At the eleventh hour, sitting there talking with her, her father became quite sure that they had done the wrong thing; that he regretted the decision to operate. But he would not go back on it; would not question the advice of the doctors whose judgement was in favour of the operation. That was something which he simply could not do. The first operation – it was one of two – was a success, but left Fatima very weak. She did not survive the second.

Pride is perhaps one of the biggest stumbling blocks to such a recantation, particularly if the decision was made very publicly and very certainly, even aggressively. It can take a long and careful process of negotiation before a formula is found which will make it possible for someone in this situation to back-track; and, indeed, which will enable the others involved in the decision to accept it also. When someone is being driven into this kind of corner, clutching the poor thin rags of her pride around her, it is simply no good to bulldoze in saying, 'Well, you've made a mistake, and we might as well admit it.' Nor, on the other hand, is it helpful to take at face value the, 'I can't *possibly* go back now,' not when you are aware she badly needs to consider seriously that very possibility of changing her mind. Your friend may not, apparently, want you to question her inability to change her mind, or to suggest that a shift might be possible. But as a friend, rather than a yes-man, you might well need to do just that. Maybe she will, finally, end up with the decision she began with. But at least she will have thrashed it out fully, she will not be left with that nagging suspicion that, perhaps, she might have done the right thing after all, had she but thought it through once more.

On those occasions – fortunately infrequent – when we have had to change our car, I have gone through precisely this process with my husband. I don't know how it is, but there seems to be some kind of collusion between motor manufacturers, that when two similar cars are on the market, both are the perfect model but for just one or two totally necessary features – which, of course, the rival possesses. And the rival, for its part, has everything which is required – except a couple of features which, for safety or comfort, are indispensable, and which are, needless to say, standard to every other model. So we talk through the pros and cons. We make lists of desirable features in order of importance. We go and talk solemnly to salesmen, who stun us with eloquent, entirely predictable though largely incomprehensible accounts of why *their* model is the safe/comfortable/economical/reliable one. Finally, we take a decision and hand over a cheque; I go thankfully to bed, only to be awakened three hours later by my husband grunting and tossing fretfully, convinced that he has done the wrong thing and that he must ring the bank tomorrow and stop that cheque. At worst, a further visit to the showrooms and yet another test drive becomes necessary. Generally, we emerge pretending not to be in the least embarrassed, sticking to the original decision.

On one occasion this was not the case. After going through our customary dithers, we were fixed on the new car. Then my son rang with incontrovertible evidence – I cannot remember what it was – about the superior safety of the rival. By that time, the very prospect of going back to those salesmen had become too embarrassing to be conceivable. It took some long and agonised conversations, reassuring ourselves as to the reasonableness of our doubts and uncertainties, the undeniable fact that we had not previously known all the facts (as if anyone ever did), and the total unimportance to our future lives of the opinion of a couple of car salesmen, before we could check out the new story and change our minds. It was our self-respect which was at stake. Of such thorny decisions are our lives, it sometimes seems, made up. . . . It is a good thing that new (or rather, new secondhand) cars are needed so rarely.

I laugh at my husband over the great and recurrent 'car trauma'. If he were writing this, he would instantly respond with an account of my no less agonised (and rather less rational) 'committee phobia'. The dithers over cars, after all, have a solid rational basis. It is hard to decide between a reputation for safety and one for reliability; or between a catalytic converter and a fifth gear. My dread and loathing of committees has no such concrete basis; I just hate them. I have, despite a committed lack of co-operation, ended up on a couple of committees. Again and again, I solemnly make the decision that *this* time, I will go. Sometimes, some unavoidable 'reason why not' emerges to save me from the meeting, such as a change of date to one which I genuinely cannot make. If no such alibi emerges, my unfortunate husband has to produce appropriately soothing noises, ones which will not serve to further wind me up, as, going upstairs to change, I descend into the depths of irrational panic.

Finding the right 'noises' to make in this situation is a skill acquired, often, over time. A friend who is willing to give support – including, at times, challenge – at such times does run a personal risk. Someone making a tough decision often needs a scapegoat, someone to be angry with. It is a highly necessary self-defence, taking some of the pain of self-blame away at a time when we are most vulnerable. But it can be difficult for the friend.

Some of these situations can be funny in retrospect – but very far from funny, at the time, to the victim of the panic or the indecision. Nevertheless, those of us who are prone to such changes of heart can learn through our own experience to distance ourselves, to some extent, from what is happening. We learn to acknowledge that this is a situation where there is no ideal, perfect choice, that we do find it hard to take responsibility for a decision in such a situation – but that we nevertheless have to brace ourselves to do the best we can and live with the consequences. After all, we are only human, and fallible, and the more often we can manage a wry smile at our own fallibility, the happier we – and those close to us – will be. I frequently find myself muttering one of my favourite Shakespeare quotations: 'Lord, what fools these mortals be.' That is Puck, in *A Midsummer Night's Dream*. I think he had a point.

8 | *Mourning the decision*

'I just wished things could have been different.'

'God I am so down, and putting a happy face on when I can for my kids and friends and family . . . Can I really go on like this?'

Most of us have said, or have heard others say, 'That was the time when I learnt who my *real* friends were.' Those are times of testing, when giving support ceases to be really quite a pleasant undertaking, with a little warm glow of self-esteem easing our way in the role of 'loving friend'. One such time of testing, without doubt, is in those weeks and months after a major decision – or indeed a death – when the sharp agony, the concentrated energy, of the decision-taking is over, and there is only the greyness of living with the consequences stretching out into an indefinite future. This can be a time of real bewilderment: so often, coming up to a major change in life, we think, 'Oh, I'll be so glad when it's all over' – and then we find that life is not as tidy as that; it is not all over. We have simply moved into the next stage of the long struggle.

As always, people vary and their needs vary. Maybe at this point, wrung out by the whole agonised saga, we will want to put it firmly behind us, to say, 'That's over now; I'm not going to think about it any more.' Each of us has to respond in our own way to our own experience, and our friends have to respect that, and not try to force us into or out of grief or anger. But however we respond to a major decision or bereavement, somewhere within us the effects of that landmark in our life will be visible. There is probably nothing dramatic to signal the transition – indeed, it would often be a great deal easier if there were. But the person who comes out is not quite the same as the person who went in, and that is something which we and our closest friends are likely to discover over time. The discovery can be destructive, or creative, or – most likely – both.

Tina had no illusions about it all being over after the abortion. There was no room in her head or heart for such illusions. Each time I reread the sections of the diary following the abortion, I am held afresh by the hugeness and the inescapability of this grief and pain. How do you live with the loss of a child you love so much; a child you need to hold, to protect, pouring our your own strength and love to strengthen your child, to make your child whole? How do you live with the aching emptiness of arms which can never be filled – not filled with *that* child, that living being whom you have known within your own body? And how, above all, do you live with that bitter separation when it is by your own act; when underneath the grief of bereavement is the muted but constant beat of the drum saying that this need not have been; that there was a choice; that perhaps it would have worked out all right? How do you cope when you keep imagining that moment, several years hence, when you could have said to your partner, 'Just think, we might have decided not to have him'; when you cannot help fantasising about the fulfilled, happy life which might have been?

But this is a life which is not, and cannot be. What remains is to live with the raw agony of the open wound, conscious always that friends and family need to be protected from too much knowledge of so great and unmanageable a pain. A friend of mine, Annette, whilst being treated (successfully) for cancer, found herself almost impossibly drained by the need to support her friends through her own pain. These friends found their grief and fear and anger incredibly difficult to handle. So either Annette had to conceal the horrors of her situation in their presence – as Tina had to do with her daughters and parents – or she had to support her friends as they came to terms with their own emotional responses to Annette's possible death. Again and again, it is the one who is most in need who is the one most able to give; but the cost to that person can be incalculable.

It can be utterly exhausting to be the friend of someone coping with the aftermath of decision – with the bereavement involved in the 'might have beens'. To hear your friend going over the same ground again and again, retaking in memory the same decisions, assuring herself – yet again – that there really was no alternative. Screaming out – again – about the injustice of it all; demanding to know *why* – why it had to be like this. Why me? Why him? Why her? Is there no place in this mad universe of whirling, mindless atoms, of bitter, arbitrary cruelty and indifference, for love and justice and compassion? To help a friend through one such dark night can seem endless. It taxes our emotional resilience and – difficult though it may be to admit – our patience; it grinds us with a sense of desperate inadequacy as we long to find the right words, the words which can give release – even while knowing that no such words can be found. But to be present to a friend, undemanding and open, through a whole series of these conversations is far harder, and yet necessary. We cry to God for aid, and sometimes in the darkness and the horror, in the deepest places of despair, we find comfort. But such moments of direct grace are rare – manna in the wilderness, not daily bread. We cry for aid – and how can aid come but through our sisters and brothers? Because we love, we have to respond, even when the going gets tough and tedious, and however halting and inadequate and sometimes bungling our responses are.

I preach here what I do not practise. In a way, it is never possible fully to practise this 'being present' for one another, because there is no end to the need. And it is simply self-destructive to flog ourselves to death: we need to know and to respect our own personal limits, our own need for comfort and nurture and fun. However hideous the situation of your friend, sometimes you need to give yourself permission to forget all about it for a spell, or at least to try to forget. Permission to go and do something completely different, something which you need or want to do for your own sake. When we give ourselves space in this way, we come back refreshed and renewed, bringing with us a breath of fresh air.

Nevertheless, I firmly believe in the centrality of real commitment to each other, however it is expressed. I have a friend who was betrayed, unspeakably betrayed by her lover and some of her closest friends and colleagues. That betrayal struck at her deepest convictions about faith and the way that faith demands to be expressed in action. It struck at her belief in human beings, and the kinds of relationship which most express and fulfil our humanity.

The lesson which I learned from this dear friend, a woman of courage and honesty and commitment, was the centrality of good faith. Do not betray. We tend to treat friendship very lightly. Most of us have a kind of inbuilt safety device, protecting us against investing too much in any one person; that safety device is often itself the product of betrayal which we have experienced in the past. Yet we need to be able to love and to trust, to penetrate into those strongest parts of ourselves where God is nakedly present and at work.

The crucifixion narratives give us some of the most powerful images of betrayal and of trust. Much of the sheer horror of the night of Gethsemane lies in the failure of the disciples to be with Jesus in his greatest need: first by sleeping in the garden, and then by Peter's threefold denial. There can be few more compelling stories of utter abandoned loneliness than that of Jesus going forward to his torture, trial and execution alone, his friends not present. The resurrection is the resurrection not only of the body but of trust, encapsulated in Peter who goes forward knowing, with every fibre of his being, the centrality of faithfulness. The crucifixion story tells also of friends who did stay, even though their presence could do nothing to alter the situation: the Marys and John, present at the cross, through it all.

Simply being present for our friends, both in crisis and in endless grey emptiness: it matters.

I have been fortunate, over the years, in meeting women and men who are active in working either in British inner cities or in situations of war and human rights abuse further afield. Their work manifests a basic commitment to the value and loveworthiness of human beings, unrewarding and unromantic and indeed unattractive as such work often is. Loving each other as we are, and being present for each other in our most difficult moments: this is the real stuff of being human. Christianity is, after all, an incarnational faith. It is about a God who becomes human – a God who enters us at Pentecost, becomes part of our lives. More to the point, our struggles and our potential become part of God's life.

This raises some practical questions. Just how do we set about 'being present' for our friends? What does that mean in practice? As always there is no one recipe, nor is there any one way of coping for those in grief. Tina knew what she needed: it was to hold Jamie, to talk with him, and she tackled that need in the most direct way. It was a way which must have seemed odd, maybe worrying, even slightly morbid to her family and friends. But she did what she needed to do with a straightforwardness which I admire. Jamie was alive to Tina and she talked with him. In the little shrine she created in her living room, in the ornament which she called 'Jamie', she gave him physical presence and space in the family home. She was acting by what was real to her at the time, and it would have been meaningless, as well as cruel and damaging, to thrust either twentieth-century rationalism or religious doctrines at her. It is not always easy to respect other people's realities, but at such times of vulnerability, it is urgently important.

The beliefs which are strongest in us are those rooted deeply in our being. Times of bitter grief and trauma, when we are almost literally 'beside ourselves', are not necessarily the times when we are in a position to respond, out of our own selves, to alternative perspectives which others wish to share with us. Indeed, we already have enough to do at such times, with the shape of the world changing around us. Tina had to come to terms with a new self: she was no longer the same person as she had been three months earlier. She was now a woman who had given life to a child, a son, who had deeply loved that son, and who had – in her own eyes – killed him. It brought a sense of guilt which could not simply be argued away. Tina had discovered in herself vast capacities for strength, for love, for ruthlessness and for hurt, which she had never known she possessed. She was operating now in a world which had changed: a world in which the worst *could* happen, the most impossible decisions *could* be asked of her. It was a world in which the boundaries of right and wrong had become blurred or, most terrifying of all, meaningless. She had discovered an aspect of life which was all dark: in which to exist was to be in pain, with no comfort anywhere. For her there was no justice and no healing anywhere, even from those from whom such healing and justice are to be expected – family, the doctors, God. The wounds were gaping raw; oceans of bewilderment, grief and anger had no established boundaries.

Tina needed time, and she needed somehow to protect the nakedness of her hurt, to contain those surging, incomprehensible emotions. And so she created her little shrine, she talked with Jamie. Perhaps it looked like escapism but it was not. Far from it. Tina was acknowledging and tending to her own needs in the best way she could. The most important thing for all her friends was to recognise and respect the nature of that struggle.

The way Tina handled her reaction to the abortion was the polar opposite of Clare, who insisted on the adoption of her brain-damaged child. Her response at the time, following the final adoption, was tacitly to forbid any mention of it. The decision was taken, the child gone, now the one necessity was to tend to the needs of the remaining children, for whose sake – ostensibly – the decision had been taken. But just recently I met Clare's sister. She had seen her sister again after a lapse of some years, and Clare had told her that there is never a day in which she does not think of her child. The older children are immaculately, anxiously – over-anxiously? – cared for and loved. But the loss, which was fiercely buried at the time, has returned to haunt her.

Tina needed to talk with Jamie, to explain her decision and assure him of her love. She did that, imaginatively, over months. Perhaps Clare has the same need, unfulfilled, with her child. Perhaps one day that child will come in search of his natural mother, and that deeply painful, but potentially creative, conversation can take place. Or perhaps Clare will continue to carry an unhealed wound. I hope not, but it can happen. I was reminded of Clare not long ago when talking with a friend about the death of her fiancé, and about the failure of her subsequent marriage. Years after both bereavement and divorce, she had entered a healing session. In the course of it, she had ended by shouting, screaming, weeping out her anger and grief against both fiancé and former husband – emotions she had no idea she was carrying. She did so in the presence of a very skilled and experienced healer, and of others who held and encouraged her through the session. It was cathartic. Such sessions can be enormously powerful for good, provided that they are skilfully and sensitively conducted.

I suspect that the aftermath of the abortion was a very difficult time for Tina's friends. She did not want to be consoled by words of comfort which could never quite touch the pain; yet she could not be her normal, naturally light-hearted self. She needed to put up barriers against too much hurt, and the barriers showed. Her friends needed to beware of the unwittingly painful remark – yet who knows what would touch a nerve? It is difficult: you badly want to be around for your friend in her need, to listen when she wants to talk or to encourage her into a bit of laughter and fun when she is able – but how can you foresee either moment? You can't always be hovering on the doorstep, listening for tears or sensing potential laughter. Life would be much simpler if we could timetable our moods: suitable allocations of trauma-time, being-daft-time, serious-conversation-time, and so on. Trauma-time, I think, should preferably be switched from its current peak, the dark, endless early hours of the morning, to the light of day.

What is possible for us, as friends, depends largely on our own circumstances – whether we live round the corner or the other end of the country, and on the extent of our own everyday commitments. But I have found that frequent and matter-of-fact contact is of infinite value. I recently read the obituary of a prominent and deeply-loved Quaker. One significant memory of her was her habit of sending regular postcards to those she knew to be in difficulties. Not highly meaningful ones, exuding designer helpfulness; but simple, brief, often wryly humorous little messages, letting people know that they were in her thoughts; that they and their wellbeing mattered to her – not as a flash in the pan, but over time. Telephone calls can serve a similar purpose. And so, of course, can company: again, undemonstratively offered, whether it be a periodic invitation to a casual meal, or joining forces on shopping expeditions, or taking the children off someone's hands for the day.

I have never forgotten one time when I was feeling very battered, a much cherished dream just having fallen apart. A friend realised that I was in a bad state and rang up out of the blue, asking me to join her and her daughter in a visit to an exhibition next morning. I rarely go to museums, and would not have picked that exhibition, personally; but I was dreading another day alone, and the fact that she asked me, that she wanted to include me in the outing, meant an enormous amount. So, on another occasion, did the unexpected appearance of an audio tape in the post, sent by friend who knew I was unhappy, and who thought the piece of music she had recorded for me would speak to my condition. It did – but even more helpful was the fact of her having taken the trouble to record and send it.

There are all sorts of ways of being there, being present

for someone; what matters above all is that it is frequent enough, and relaxed enough, that our company will give her the opportunity to weep, to scream, to laugh or to be nothing-in-particular as the need arises for her. There is nothing more unhelpful than to be weighed down by the presence of friends who are expecting us to want to 'talk about it', or on the other hand who are thinking that we really should have got over it by now.

And, of course, when we get there it is quite probable that we will be met by coldness, an empty unresponsiveness, or active irritability. That is hard to take; 'I don't know why I bothered to go,' we say or think. 'She didn't seem to want me.' Earlier, I referred to the way in which the world had changed for Tina, becoming a place in which the worst could happen, in which justice and healing were not forthcoming. When the worst happens, we often – maybe always – need to be angry. Why has this happened? How has it been allowed? – why have not 'they' prevented it? Or now that it has happened, why can they not take the pain away?

These questions are not wholly rational, though they spring out of the very basic sense of justice and demand for security which undergird much of our rational thought. When we are badly hurt, we need to react: to kick out in outrage against that which has hurt us; to scream, maybe even to inflict hurt on others, to see them wince as the dagger pierces them. It is a terribly lonely place, this bewildering place of incurable pain. Our fear and our loneliness and our hurt can uncover savagery in us which we never dreamt was there. That may sound unpleasant and may conflict entirely with the picture we have of ourselves, the picture we present to our friends, the picture they present to us. Experience shows that it tends to be harder for women than for men to admit to anger and the capacity for violence. In prison, men tend to fight one another; women are far more prone to self-mutilation, often in hidden, unacknowledged ways. Neither is ideal; but the anger and violence which is kept festering, unacknowledged, in the dark, tends to be in the long term far more damaging to ourselves and to others. Far better to have it out in the open, even by lashing out at an innocent friend, than to let it fester and to risk ultimately turning it against ourselves or against others with all the added venom of a long-festering wound.

This is not fun for the friend. To be hit, hard, precisely when we are trying to help, is not easy. Especially when the aggression accumulates over a period of time. In some ways it is harder to be present for a close friend than for one who is more distant – at least, I find it so. That is partly because it can be harder to respond adequately to what a friend is saying and feeling – maybe we know too much, maybe we are too aware of the unspoken complications to be able to find words. And partly it is because of our built-in selfishness: the resentment which, however much we love, can build up when our own joys and griefs are sidelined by the urgency of our friend's need. Of course, when I have found myself building up that kind of Eeyore-like, 'Doesn't matter about me' resentment, I sometimes realise afterwards that I was miscalculating the situation; that my friend would have welcomed hearing my current batch of problems or minor triumphs, partly as a relief from her own, and partly because she had a fund of generous love and concern which needed to be used. I blunder a great deal, particularly with those who are closest to me. I think that is probably typical – that we can be most 'useful' to those in difficulty who are not close personal friends. But when we are in grief, we need our friends; we need them to stick to us; we need that stickability even through our worst moodiness.

Indeed, we sometimes test out their friendship, unconsciously, by putting them through such tests. That is certainly the case with my family. My daughter acknowledges now that I was a prime focus of her anger and indeed hatred; but that her security was dependent upon knowing that her bitter tongue would not drive me permanently away. Maybe it is the human equivalent of those psychotherapeutic techniques which encourage patients to disgorge their anger by being as violent and wildly messy as possible – using punchballs to thump, china to smash, paint to throw. Well, I think my daughter needed to use me as a punchball; she needed to be able to vent that anger safely.

I do not want to give the impression that the aftermath of a decision such as Tina's will suddenly turn you, or your friend, into a permanently irritable, angry, bewildered person, who could do with a prominent health warning placarded on her chest: 'Beware: unsafe to know.' Absolutely not, for this is a self-perception which needs to be avoided when we are in grief. It is very easy to slip into seeing ourselves as permanent bores at best; at worst, as monsters who pollute by their very presence. We saw earlier the need to differentiate between the responsibility which we must take for our decisions, and the damaging, self-mutilating guilt which cuts us off from our fellow humans and sucks dry our capacity for love and creativity. One central role for our friend is to show us, by her continued presence and support, by her nonjudgemental responses to our outpourings or bad temper, that we are still lovable: that we are not marked off as infectiously unlucky or untouchable sinners.

Again, it is not always easy to walk this particular tightrope. For when someone is in pain, and lashing out verbally from that pain, she needs to know that her friend respects her. It does not help if we simply write off all these pain-filled words as the outpourings of delirium: produce some soothing verbal formula and a cup of tea, and she will be better. Those outpourings express her sense of the world where she is now, the world as it appears to her in the depth of her pain. That has to be respected, not humoured, patted on the head. But, equally, we need to avoid responding to such expressions of anger or grief or bitterness as her final and decided view of life, to be discussed and countered with careful rationality. Hold him or her, whether physically or emotionally; hear her and respect her; affirm her value, her loveableness; be ready to dissolve passion into laughter if the opportunity arises; but never belittle and never judge. It is not our right.

And be ready to play! Another glowing memory, of not so long ago: I was again feeling unhappy, churned up, angry – I do not know what about, but it was brimming up inside me, physically present. I needed to *scream!* So I seized a friend, mercifully on hand, and we took the dog out for a short, brisk walk along the river. It was February, cold and damp, and she egged me on as I went roaring after some innocent ducks, placidly snoozing on the bank – chasing them, shouting at the top of my voice. Highly reprehensible, but at the time it was wonderful. I went back indoors with a spring in my step and laughter in my heart, to the benefit of those around me, who otherwise were destined to suffer a day of my intense irritability. In fact, that was a wonderful relationship. At the time my friend was in a bad way, nearing the suicidal. I would zestfully encourage some of her dottier actions, which were to her what duck chasing was to me that day. It is good to go mad, now and then. Far better than churning up inside and finally either hitting yourself or those around you. In a way, Tina's little 'shrine', and her ornament of Jamie, was not dissimilar. To a firmly rational mind, they looked absurd, superstitious, morbid. But she needed to give some sort of expression to her overflowing love for Jamie. She acted out her love, as I acted out my anger with the unfortunate ducks that day.

The way we mourn a decision is, of course, immensely influenced by our response over time to the rightness of that decision. Grief and regret for the might-have-beens Tina certainly felt; but mercifully she was never afflicted by those corrosive 'if only's' which come with the conviction of a tragically wrong choice. That is where the real anger and potential for despair are to be found. Tina had to live with a new, an expanded self but, in many ways, it was a stronger, fuller self which she had discovered. It was a frightening self in some ways, in its capacity for such ruthlessness. But that ruthlessness was the product of bottomless love, and this she discovered, too.

It is very different when the self which we discover, or the self to whose promptings we agree, is one which revolts or shames us. If the horror at what we discover about ourself is severe, then we may need professional help to come to terms with it, to learn to live with this shadow side of ourself. But again, what we probably need from our friends is acceptance. This is not a mindless condoning of that which is so horrible to us: it does not help, if I have done a thing which I know to be vile, if my friends say, 'There, there, it's not so bad really.' All that is likely to produce is my loss of respect for my friends. But it does help if they can continue to love me through the horror, to acknowledge my loveworthiness as a person, despite this shadow which is part of me.

And if we do bring our shadows into the light, speaking about the actions of which we are most ashamed, we may find that much of their horror evaporates. I have certainly been in the position of listening to friends' confidences, as they voice things about themselves which make them creep with horror and shame; and their 'crimes' have sounded – not trivial, but so small in relation to the significance attached to them! It is quite hard, sometimes, to give adequate weight to the significance of such memories, yet to find words in which to put them into a different perspective, outside the foetid heat of the enclosed imagination. Our ability to do this, to accept and love one another through it all, neither judging nor condoning the fault, depends upon our familiarity with their own shadows. We are better able to be good friends if we know ourselves to be capable of words and deeds which, in theory, we would deplore.

And if we have taken decisions out of that which is weakest in ourselves, then somehow we need to be able to reclaim that stronger self – not to sink into a despairing sense that that fearful, selfish being is all that there is to me. There is always a way forwards: not a way back to where we or those people affected by our decisions came from, for we can never go back there, not after a major decision, a major grief. But we can always go on and find new potential in both ourselves and others – as Peter did, reclaimed by Jesus' renewed trust in him, 'Feed my sheep.' Even when the consequences of our action reverberate, affecting ourselves and others whom we love, there is always a way forward. But it does take courage to know that and to seek it out; and we do need the strength, the support and the affirmation of our friends.

9 ‖ A changed identity

'I'll never know if what I did was right. I can just hope it was.'

We can rarely know if a decision which we made in the hope of doing good or averting worse evil was 'right' or 'wrong'. In a way, those words 'right' and 'wrong' even lose their meaning. We act with the wisdom given to us, out of the necessity of the moment. Sometimes we act in a way which hurts ourselves or others now, in the hope of avoiding worse hurt later; sometimes we risk the future for the sake of the present. Both are difficult choices. But it is often a long time before we can come to this acceptance that we have done what we have done; and that now all we can do is work with the consequences. We can just hope that good can grow out of what we did, or we can dedicate what we did to God, asking for God's help in going forward. Either way, we need somehow to relinquish the agonising over that decision, the endless nightmare of, 'Did I do right?' 'I think I did wrong.' Some people do not have this difficulty – they are able, or they have learnt, to accept their own decisions as either right or at any rate as a *fait accompli*: such acceptance, provided that it does not prevent them from ever acknowledging themselves to have been mistaken, is a great liberation.

It was a long time before Tina was able to relinquish her confusion. Nor could she do so in any cut and dried, once-and-for-all way. It is a long process. We can rarely chart its process, but gradually, over time, we realise that we are no longer in the place of desolation where we once were. Tina worked from a position of strength. Agonising as her decision was, she took it out of love, out of her strength rather than her weakness. The self who took that decision was a self she could thereafter live with. And she acknowledged her grief and confusion and guilt: not to her family, because they were unable to help her, to a large degree; but to her diary and to Jamie himself. The old Christian language of repentance, confession and absolution can sound alien, full of an authoritarianism which is a block to many of us. But the process of feeling the hurt, of painfully, honestly naming it and offering it up to the one who has been hurt, actually or in imagination, asking to be cleansed: this process is a powerful one. It is the principle which underlies that Christian tradition. In a way, it underlies the policy of the Probation Service, of helping offenders to acknowledge the human consequences of their crimes, and then to meet with those whom they have wronged, in some way seeking to make reparation to them. Over time, Tina came alive again. She and Joe were gradually able to talk about Jamie together, even to laugh together about aspects of the past. The future came to hold promise once more, rather than merely the threat of long endurance.

It does become possible to relinquish the past: not forgetfully, but letting it *be* the past. I have just been thinking, with some amusement, about one of the most committed members of the 'if-only' school of thought in the Old Testament: Moses. 'Why have you landed me in this mess, God? Why couldn't you have left us safely in Egypt? It wasn't exactly a bed of roses, but it was better than wandering around the wilderness with no food or drink or future – and a right unthankful mob of people into the bargain . . .'. Moses regretted, had doubts, was angry with God. But there was no going back: and he was able to avoid being incapacitated by those doubts. He went on, looking for a future even when that future looked most unhopeful. A bit like my gallant prostitute friend Karen, who was able to forgive the fates, or herself, or the authorities, or whoever it was that landed her in her various disasters, and to go on, laughing at the sheer mad complexity of her situation. Karen was no Christian, but I can most surely give thanks for the grace of God in her life.

The process of mourning the decision, and of learning to live with the self who made that decision, can take longest of all for those who have come to believe that that decision was a mistaken one. That was one burden which Tina did not have to carry. I have met this dilemma most cruelly in the lives of those who abort or divorce too precipitately. It is harder to acknowledge such regret when the parents decide *not* to abort, and then have to live with a severely handicapped child. Guilt and regret can be like a knife twisting deep inside, a physical weight upon the shoulders, a shame which renders us less able to love and be with others, because we regard ourselves as so worthless, so unlovable. The sharpness of the regret can make us irritable and surly, embittered by having to live with our unloved selves and the wrong we have done ourselves – and, quite probably, others. It is a prison which we resent, longing to get away from it, to get away from ourselves, from everything and everyone who reminds us of that which we have lost.

Clare, who had her mentally handicapped child adopted, is still mourning that decision, though I do not think she has actually said to herself that that choice was the wrong one. But the making of the decision nearly broke her marriage. Her husband, Martin, resisted the adoption with all his power. After it had gone through, he found it almost impossible to be with her, to go to work, to be at home – to be with himself. Suicide was a real possibility, as was a car accident, so entirely preoccupied was he by his grief. Nor would I have been surprised had he walked out on his job and headed north to where his own family came from, taking his remaining children with him. His grief was savage, uncommunicative. I have no idea what his own support mechanisms were; I hope he had male friends to whom he could voice his bitterness. I hope there were people who could simply be alongside him – silent over a pint in the pub, or in a tramp over the Downs, people who were not deterred in their affection for him by his abruptness, his turbulently brooding silences. Martin's actions, his manner, the intensity of his silence all voiced it: this was no un-acknowledged grief. The intensity of his mourning has passed, now, though I am quite sure that the wound will never fully heal.

In a way, Martin's is a less destructive experience than regret is for those who cannot even acknowledge it to themselves. These are people who carry with them an empty hopelessness, a nameless depression and flatness. They see themselves as the victims of fate, unable to change their destiny, or to challenge their own role as the plaything of forces beyond their control. All we can do is love them, let them know they are loved, and trust that in time something will bring the hidden wound to the light, where a process of healing may begin. And maybe we can sometimes challenge, very gently, this victim role. To attack it directly is highly unlikely to help: such a challenge, indeed, simply works to reinforce the sense of powerlessness in an aggressive and all-powerful world, which has to be passively endured. I have made that mistake, more than once. But it is possible to underline, gently, the ways in which your friend is not a passive victim. The ways in which she is strong, is taking command of her situation. The ways, indeed, in which she is demonstrably loved and lovable. If in making a major decision she was acting out of her weak or least lovable self, it can be hard indeed for her to climb out of the pit of identification with that self. But it can be done – gradually, imperceptibly; reinforced by friends who, like the father in the parable of the prodigal son, go out to greet and welcome and affirm the self who is, slowly, coming home.

I remember one father and daughter with whom I worked for a while. They were brought to our attention at the hospital by the stepmother, who could no longer handle the girl's constant weepiness, with which her husband Maurice, chronically indecisive, was wholly unable to cope. Whatever she said, the child would dissolve into tears. When she was three, she had been out for an evening walk in the woods with her natural mother who had been taken by an acute asthma attack. The child had finally run to a nearby cottage for help. The mother was whisked into hospital. She never saw her again. When there was obviously no hope left, the doctors had to ask the father's consent to turn off the life support machines. Neither father nor daughter had ever talked about the whole traumatic episode; both had been carrying an intolerable burden of guilt for their part in the wife and mother's death – all those if-only's: 'If only I had gone for help sooner', 'If only I had asked for another twenty-four hours before they switched it off . . .'. The stepmother, in due course, had done all she could to get beneath their deep-rooted unhappiness and try to strengthen the vital, laughing people she knew were buried underneath the guilt and grief. She held them through some very bad times; but she knew she was really only putting sticking-plaster on the wound. It had to be acknowledged and brought out into the open, so that father and daughter could talk together about what had happened, and about their individual and shared responsibilities.

If someone is so overwhelmed by one decision, however traumatic, it may well be that this is building on an earlier lack of self-respect and self-confidence, however irrational. That sense that, 'Whatever I do will be the wrong thing', 'Whatever I do will hurt someone', can grow out of an overwhelming sense of responsibility for others, a sense of failure and guilt for not being able to carry other people's burdens. It can be good to tackle that huge burden of over-responsibility in respect of one difficult decision, working out the actual limits of responsibility, and learning to say, 'The rest is not my problem'. But learning that lesson is a long and difficult task, and very often it means going back over whatever it was in the past which has laid this burden upon us. In just that way, Maurice and his weeping daughter had to go back far beyond any current problems to find the roots of their unhappiness and insecurity, the guilt which they had taken upon themselves.

Thinking back over my experience, those people who have been impelled into a process of self-examination have been pushed into it less often directly by the burden of over-responsibility which they carry, than by the oppression of a continual grief which goes along with it. To have to take a decision, however small, means deciding *against* something: it means losing something, and that can play upon a long-established hurt. Often it can go back to the oldest loss of all: that insufficiency of love in early childhood which can through the rest of life leave a deep-rooted insecurity and a heart like dry soil yearning for water. Karen did not react this way. Her childhood had been lacking in every conceivable amenity and security; but she remained zestfully determined to pour into her arid and unpromising surroundings her own unquenchable and loving spirit. Others cannot respond as she did: they hobble through life, lamed by early experience. Or, unexpectedly, the past comes leaping out to stab them. A man I worked with for a while, Albert, who had taken early retirement from teaching, was thus stabbed. He believed that he had thought through his decision to retire, and had taken into account the difficulties of adjusting to a new role. In fact, he was devastated by the change. His old identity stripped away, he found himself in an uncharted desert, knowing neither himself nor any realities around him. Grief and confusion he had never realised he was carrying were there, ready to fill the empty spaces. Questions of which he had never dreamed, about the purpose of his life and the nature of his relations with other people, were waiting to ambush him. Not only was he being forced to discover his own changed identity, but he had also a different status in the outside world: he was no longer a practising teacher, but a 'retired person'. Living with the consequences of his decision to retire was no simple matter for Albert: it was a case almost of beginning again, becoming acquainted with himself and the world.

We talk of people having a mid-life crisis; it can indeed be an incredibly sharp, painful – and exciting – crisis. Or it can be a far slower, subtler transition, a gradual emergence of questions needling in the back of the mind, pressing for attention. It can be confusing for our friends, as they wonder what is happening to us – suddenly we are no longer the person they had known. Albert's wife undoubtedly found it an incredibly difficult period. On top of the known hazards of him being around all day in a way which she had not previously experienced – and she worked from home, using the front room as an office – came his uncertain moods, his need to be alone yet his fear of loneliness and, increasingly, his need to be somewhere else, to move physically into the kind of environment which better fitted the person he was becoming.

Marriages can break under the strain of this kind of transition, often though not necessarily precipitated by retirement, redundancy or change of job. Drink or other addictions can come to be a problem. It is often good for both partners to have friends to whom they can talk, including someone to whom they can talk as a couple, voicing their confusions and resentments in the presence of, and speaking to, an impartial third person. Occasionally, such a situation develops naturally in relation to a personal friend, known and trusted by both. It is an extraordinarily difficult and delicate situation to be in, and that friend will probably come out of it far from certain whether he or she has done good or ill by being present. I have never offered to play such a part – indeed, it is a quite remarkably unpleasant role, to my mind, and I avoid it like the plague! It is a great deal easier, I find, to fill this kind of role with people who are not personal friends. One has a greater impartiality, has less personally invested in the outcome of the conflict, and so is better able to hear and reflect what is being said. Nevertheless, I have on a couple of occasions been asked by one or other of a pair of personal friends to be present in this sort of way. All one can do is to try to help each reflect, as clearly and fully as possible, what they are actually thinking and feeling, how they are seeing the situation, to the other.

It is always a bit of a shock to see how dramatically different any situation can appear to two individuals involved in it. And so often also, partners are unable to hear the pain in the other's voice, interpreting it instead as criticism of themselves. I have spent hours with each 'side', both hearing – with head and heart – their perceptions of the situation and trying to describe to them how it seems to the other. Anger can frequently be the response which you receive in this situation, even from friends or clients who have asked for your presence. Yet respect can also be born out of your willingness to give voice to the unpalatable.

The process of coming to terms with a difficult decision, once made, can be very similar to the process of making that decision. Not always, of course: there can quite simply be an immense and lasting relief after the decision has been made. But if it has been a significant choice – the life-changing questions of birth and death, marriage and work – then it is almost certain to have raised questions and uneasinesses which, at some stage and in some form, are likely to raise their heads. Those questions may very well reflect not only the immediately precipitating dilemma or memory: they will be inextricably interwoven with a far greater tapestry of living and loving and hating of which this one decision was but one, albeit significant, part. We should not be surprised when such periods of questioning and pain hit, dramatically or quietly, ourselves or our friends. They are part of being human.

Friendship is about being there for our friends when they need the solidity of nonjudgemental acceptance; or maybe the fellowship of a mind willing to ask questions alongside them; when they need a human punchball to vent their anger on – and quite likely a pair of human arms to hug them tightly, whether actually or metaphorically; perhaps when they need someone willing honestly to agree that a decision was wrong – yet able to show their love and respect for the person who made that decision. Someone, too, who will not make assumptions about what our responses to crises or problems 'ought to be'.

Early in my career, I remember going along to one bereaved household. I was full of the milk of human kindness and a glowing desire to help. The widower opened the door. 'B... off,' he said succinctly. 'We don't need you.' Fair enough. But there are times when companionship is needed, an infinity of ways in which our friends need us and we need them – to weep and scream and laugh. It is the mixture which is healthy, and creative. Like going to visit Karen towards the end of her life, when she knew she could not live much longer; listening while she talked about her fears for the children, her longing not to have to leave them; and then going out with her to do some of the heavy shopping that she could not possibly do unaided. I remember being utterly helpless with mirth when Karen, one great balloon of laughter, got stuck in the door of my little car, in the middle of the high street, one hot summer afternoon. Good memories, of so many courageous people: all so different, responding to their crises and joys with such resilience, in an infinity of ways.

Conclusion

Books and films come to an end. The covers close, the credits roll; the threads of conflicts and dilemmas are tied together, for good or ill. There is a resolution.

Real life is not like that. Decisions and actions reverberate, in our lives and the lives of those close to us. Decisions about birth and death, about relationships and jobs, are endings – but they are also beginnings. They are moulded by our circumstances and personalities but also in turn mould them. We are changed, affected, by what we and others do and say. It is thus that we grow – and that growth can be creative or destructive. Or, most likely, it can be a mixture.

If this were a novel, the story of Tina, Joe and their family, we could give it a happy ending. For it does continue happily. Two years after the abortion, Tina conceived again. The child is strong and healthy, a boy. At Joe's insistence they have called him Jamie; this is the son for whom he has longed and that son can for Joe have only one name.

For Tina, this was a difficult decision. For her, Jamie already existed, was still alive. He had for her a very clear identity and personality. The little ornament still stands in the corner of the sitting room, the means by which Tina can communicate with her child.

But, though Jamie probably always will exist for her, Tina has been able to let him go, to cease clinging to him in grief and guilt. She has talked with him, with her diary and with others; she has prayed that, wherever he is now, he may be received with love and tenderness. Tina has been able to lay him down. She knows that she struggled to do her best not only for herself and her family but for him. He is safe.

The relationship between Joe and Tina has changed in these last years. It is closer than it was: the love, respect and trust between them is stronger. But there is also much which is not said, is not understood. The experience of the abortion was radically different for the two of them, as is shown by the choice of name for the new child. They cannot understand or enter into one another's experiences. But they are able to respect, accept and work with that different-ness, unthreatened by it.

The situation is very different for Clare, who is far from such acceptance of the loss of her child, now adopted. There was much in her own decision, and in her motivation for it, which she has never been able to acknowledge. There is much which cannot be spoken between herself and her hus-band, for whom adoption never was and never can be the right decision. Clare lives with the ghost of her child, yet is unable to speak out her confusion and guilt and grief as Tina was able to do. She cannot ask for the child's forgive-ness, and cannot receive it. This is not to say that she 're-grets' the decision. She was driven by her own necessity at the time. I think she would almost certainly do the same again, even knowing the pain it would cause. But, without 'regretting', she can grieve.

Like most of us, she is in conflict with herself. I personally believe that it is good to confront and seek, gradually, to understand the roots of our own conflict – though such a process is hard. But I also think that such self-enquiry can be overstressed, to our great damage. One of Tina's strengths is her sense of humour, her willingness to accept herself as she is, with all her limitations. She does not de-mand perfection of herself and she does not flog herself for acting within her own limits.

Tina, of course, has been more fortunate than many. Hard though it was to live with Joe's very different attitude to Jamie, she has not been subjected to indifference or active cruelty. Even in the worst times of uncertainty, when right and wrong were lost in whirling confusion, she was able to fall back on a sense of the reality of love, of caring. In such a context, she could let go of Jamie, knowing him, wherever he is, to be loved, and feeling also his love for her.

It is very different for those who have been abused, in whatever way, and whose vision of the world is based on an awareness of cruelty or, at best, indifference. This is, I think, a difference between Tina and big Karen on the one hand, and Clare and blind Anna on the other. Clare and Anna lived in a world in which fear and guilt and lonely unsupportedness were basic realities. From whatever source, Tina and Karen knew far more clearly what love and support were. This made them more able to accept their own and others' limits: to accept, to forgive and to feel forgiven.

And to laugh. A friend has described to me her sense of the presence of God as a great balloon of joy and laughter inside her – huge, buoyant, indestructible. That friend has herself known and has worked amongst terrible suffering: so here is no false complacency. In part it is a gift, this capacity for happiness – the gift of circumstances and temperament. In part, it is the fruit of courage and honesty. Tina had to struggle hard in order to emerge unembittered, still trusting, able to lay down the past and go forward, able to laugh.

All of us differ in the stories that have moulded us, the experiences to which we have been subjected, the strengths and weaknesses which we have been given. I have great difficulty with the assertion that none of us have crosses too heavy to bear. As a fact of experience, some or us are given troubles which are quite simply too heavy for us to carry as individuals. We can be broken, driven to bitterness or despair. But that simply underlines the centrality of relationship, community, companionship – there are many words for it. For that is being present for each other, in love; gently judging the other's actions maybe but never the other's self.

We cannot carry our griefs and confusions alone. We need each other. And in being present to each other we can learn and gain so much.

Also published by

Tri∧ngle

LIVING WITH ANGER
by Myra Chave-Jones

A positive view of anger and how it can be used as an important part of our lives.

FREE TO FAIL
by Russ Parker

A Christian exploration of the problems many people have with facing up to failure and its place in the spiritual life.

SEVEN FOR A SECRET THAT'S NEVER BEEN TOLD
Healing the wounds of sexual abuse in childhood
by Tracy Hansen

The moving account of a survivor of child sexual abuse working through the trauma induced by the return of re-pressed memories.

UNWORLD PEOPLE
For anyone who has felt unwanted, unusable, unloved
by Joyce Landorf Heatherley

Shows the growth of hope and faith after rejection, based on the author's own experience.

BELIEF BEYOND PAIN
by Jenny Francis
Foreword by Richard Bewes

A remarkable insight into one person's physical pain and its effect on her life, faith and relationships.

LOSING AND LIVING
Thoughts on every kind of grieving
by David M Owen

Considers a range of personal losses - from bereavement of family and friends in death to the loss of our own health, youth or job. It includes many apt and revealing quotations which speak directly of the experience of grief.

FROM WHERE I SIT
Living with disability in an able-bodied world
by Alison Davis

A disturbing, personal and often funny account of what it is really like to be disabled.

WHO'S THIS SITTING IN MY PEW?
Mentally handicapped people in the church
by Faith Bowers

Considers what the church can do for mentally handicapped people and what they bring to the church.

HOW MANY TIMES CAN YOU SAY GOODBYE?
Living with bereavement
by Jenifer Pardoe

A down-to-earth look at grief, with many everyday stories to give practical insights into what can be done to understand and help in times of bereavement.

Tri△ngle

Books
can be obtained from
all good bookshops.
In case of difficulty,
or for a complete list of our books,
contact:
SPCK Mail Order
36 Steep Hill
Lincoln
LN2 1LU
(tel: 0522 527 486)